CW00918688

Captured Behind
Japanese Lines

Captured Behind Japanese Lines

With Wingate's Chindits – Burma 1942–1945

Daniel Berke

Pen & Sword
MILITARY

First published in Great Britain in 2021 by
Pen & Sword Military
An imprint of
Pen & Sword Books Ltd
Yorkshire – Philadelphia

ISBN 978 1 39901 688 9

A CIP catalogue record for this book is
available from the British Library.

Printed and bound in the UK by CPI Group (UK) Ltd,
Croydon, CR0 4YY.

MIX
Paper from
responsible sources
FSC® C013604

Pen & Sword Books Limited incorporates the imprints of Atlas,
Archaeology, Aviation, Discovery, Family History, Fiction, History,
Maritime, Military, Military Classics, Politics, Select, Transport,
True Crime, Air World, Frontline Publishing, Leo Cooper, Remember
When, Seaforth Publishing, The Praetorian Press, Wharncliffe
Local History, Wharncliffe Transport, Wharncliffe True Crime
and White Owl.

For a complete list of Pen & Sword titles please contact

PEN & SWORD BOOKS LIMITED
47 Church Street, Barnsley, South Yorkshire, S70 2AS, England
E-mail: enquiries@pen-and-sword.co.uk
Website: www.pen-and-sword.co.uk

Or

PEN AND SWORD BOOKS
1950 Lawrence Rd, Havertown, PA 19083, USA
E-mail: Uspen-and-sword@casematepublishers.com
Website: www.penandswordbooks.com

Dedication

To my grandfather Frank, who put one foot in front of the other and didn't give up and who never lost his humanity or faith. Because of his fortitude and courage I am here, with my wife and with my children. This is my belated insufficient 'thank you' and so that my children, niece and nephews may know Frank's story.

Contents

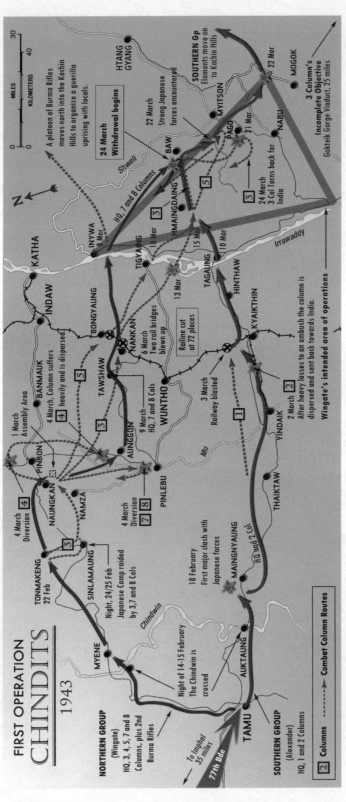

Acknowledgements

At the time I write this note of thanks to the many people who have helped and encouraged me, Myanmar, the enigmatic country at the heart of this story, is suffering. When I travelled to Myanmar in 2017, a fragile democracy had just been born and Burmese citizens had a say in their country's governance after decades of military rule. It was sadly short-lived. On 1 February 2021 the people of Myanmar woke to find that the military had seized control in a coup. Democratic leaders were arrested and, in the coming days, dozens were killed in demonstrations.

This book would not have been possible without the help of so many people in Myanmar who answered my questions, opened their homes to me and shared their stories: my knowledgeable guides Ko Soe Win and Myo Myo who opened doors and found paths; U Myo Myint and the people of Inywa; U Chow and the villagers in Waw; the family in Shwebo; Nyo Ko Naing in Katha; and a wonderful teacher, Serena Flock, who approached me, asked if I was British and spent the day showing me around Pyin Oo Lwin. So many gave up their time for me and it is my profound hope that when I return, it will be to a full democracy.

In India, my thanks go to my guide and friend Hemant Goswami who brought the past to life and explained the present as he took me and my dad through the jungles and forts where the Chindits were born, to Dr Jain of Saugar University, and Abishek Akash who took us to the Garrison Church and the forests of Patharia.

The first book I read that mentioned Frank was published by Pen & Sword, and I was delighted when they agreed to publish my book. My thanks go to Henry Wilson – who knows what it is to soldier in the jungle – for his advice and support, to my editor Pamela 'Hawkeye' Covey and to all the team at Pen & Sword.

I am very grateful to my friends Deborah Britstone (the best colleague I could ask for) and Richard Chapman QC for their support and for working through my drafts and giving me feedback and ideas, and a big thanks to the many friends who encouraged me to put pen to paper and tell Frank's story.

There are a number of former soldiers I would like to thank. First, I am very grateful to Colonel Richard Kemp, a man who has been a great inspiration to me, for writing the Foreword to this book. My grandfather suffered all his life after the war from psychological trauma. I was determined that some good should come from his suffering. James Deegan, former Regimental Sergeant Major of the Special Air Service – the most elite of all Special Forces – kindly made enquiries for me and recommended Billy MacLeod and the inspirational team at Veterans in Action as a charity for royalties from print sales of this book to support. The work done by VIA is humbling and greatly needed, and my thanks go to Billy and his team and all who purchase this book and help their work.

Captured Behind Japanese Lines is a history I share with my brothers Richard and Steven and my thanks go to them for listening to my ideas, and to my dad, Tony, for sharing in my journey and my mum, Anne, for letting him, much as she worried. I also need to thank my mum for the years spent pleading with me to do my English homework essays; it probably paid off.

This is a story I am glad my children Millie and Tal now know. As I researched and wrote about the horrific experiences faced by my grandfather, I know that they are part of my life and part of this world because of his fortitude.

I have been encouraged and supported every step of the way by my wife, soul mate and best friend Carmel. Like the heroes in this book, she has taken that step forward and volunteered as a soldier. She continues to inspire me every day.

My special thanks go to Stephen Fogden. Stephen's grandfather Arthur Leslie Howney was a Chindit who was captured and died in Rangoon. In the many years he has spent researching the grandfather he never met, Stephen has collected stories, documents, memories and information about hundreds of other Chindits. Stephen's generosity with his time, that most precious commodity, his commitment to sharing knowledge and helping descendants of Chindits has allowed me to find out more than I ever hoped for about Frank. He checked my manuscript, advised me on travel destinations and helped me to research. Above all, he keeps alive the memory of the courageous men of the Chindits.

From the Author

I have referred to Myanmar as Burma throughout this book. This is because I have used the name by which this country was known at the time my grandfather and his comrades fought there, and because that is how it is referred to in the sources I have used. For consistency, I have elected to use the same name throughout. No disrespect is meant to the people of Myanmar, many of whom opened their homes to me, ate with me, answered my questions, posed for photographs and all of whom met me with warm smiles.

Foreword

We often think of the courage fighting men must summon up when they go into battle, faced by the very real prospect of being killed or maimed. Less often we consider another extreme hazard that also confronts them: capture by a vengeful and ruthless enemy. In his 1895 poem, Rudyard Kipling evoked the horror of what might follow, suggesting that the 'young British soldier' on the plains of Afghanistan, rather than be captured and tortured, should 'roll to your rifle and blow out your brains'. Some 120 years later, British troops fighting again in the same place designed their battle tactics specifically to avoid the prospect of a soldier being isolated and taken by the Taliban.

Many British prisoners of war were appallingly treated and sometimes tortured, starved to death or murdered by their German captors in the First World War. The same fate befell some of their sons taken prisoner by the Germans in the war that followed. Yet none of this came even close to the extreme and incessant brutality meted out to those captured by the Imperial Japanese Army in the Second World War. Of 50,000 British prisoners of the Japanese, one-quarter died of starvation, disease or abuse in captivity.

By the time the author of this book's grandfather, Frank Berkovitch, and his fellow Chindits infiltrated behind enemy lines in Burma, stories of Japanese treatment of prisoners were well known. The men of the first Chindit operation underwent a highly demanding selection and training course. All knew that the mission they were preparing for was extremely dangerous and previously unproven, and that once in the Burmese jungle, there could be no hope of rescue if anything went wrong. The men were all given the opportunity to pull out, yet not one of those who passed the training chose to do so.

This stoicism was matched by the Chindits' fighting spirit and their commitment to each other and their mission. The cost of taking the fight to the enemy was high: about one-third of the 3,000 men who crossed the Chindwin River did not return. So were the stakes. Following the swift advance of Japanese troops through Burma in December 1941 and the retreat of the British forces, a belief developed that the Japanese army could not be beaten and were unequalled in jungle warfare. Retaking Burma became the longest-fought campaign of the Second World War, and one of the bloodiest. At the conclusion of the war, in Burma Allied forces had turned defeat into victory, in the words of Field Marshal Sir William Slim, who commanded the British Fourteenth Army.

The fight back against the Japanese began with the Chindits, who in 1943 carried out a daring raid deep behind enemy lines. They destroyed infrastructure and supply chains, gathered intelligence and dispelled the myth of Japanese invulnerability.

The Chindits were led by Orde Wingate, a proponent of irregular warfare, an eccentric figure and an unconventional thinker who was never afraid to challenge the accepted wisdom, including among his superiors. The sort of commander that is often disdained, despised even, in peacetime, yet becomes indispensable in war, and exactly the sort of commander that appealed to Prime Minister Winston Churchill. After Wingate was killed in Burma in 1944, in a speech in the British Parliament, Churchill said of him: 'There was a man of genius who might well have become also a man of destiny.'

Another Prime Minister, David Ben Gurion, believed that had he survived the war, Wingate would have become the first Chief of Staff of the Israel Defence Forces, a remarkable possibility for a British Christian officer. Today he is at least as well known in Israel as he is in Britain and often spoken of as the father of the IDF. In pre-state Palestine, the young Captain Wingate, an ardent backer of the re-establishment of a Jewish homeland, committed himself to supporting the Jewish population which was under frequent attack from armed Arab gangs. He set up and turned the 'Special Night Squads' into crack units capable of carrying out fast and deadly raids; an early insight into the kind of thinking that would lead him to create the Chindits.

Few would have dared to take on Wingate's task in Burma. It was an audacious undertaking to harass the Japanese behind their own front lines, resupplied entirely by air. What made him suited to this operation was not just an unconventional military mind, but a commitment to lead by example, share hardships and set the pace, doing all he asked of his men and more.

In their journey into largely uncharted territory, facing a formidable foe in the harshest terrain and climate, the men of the Chindits formed the strongest of bonds. Throughout *Captured Behind Japanese Lines* there are numerous examples of sacrifice and outstanding bravery: from the Burmese rifleman who volunteered to stay with a wounded officer and, even under torture, refused to give him up; to the RAF pilot who risked his life to land his plane in a short jungle clearing rather than leave wounded men to certain death. The Chindits' courage was remarkable. They fought against a numerically superior enemy, in the jungle, in engagements at close quarters and often hand-to-hand.

The men who were taken into captivity drew on the same reserves of courage, in utterly soul-destroying conditions. The examples of unending Japanese cruelty in this book are painful to read. Frank Berkovitch tells of the risks he and his fellow prisoners took on working parties outside the prison in order to smuggle food back to sick comrades. They did so even though they themselves were starving and even though they knew they would be brutally beaten for it. The commitment of the prisoners of war to each other was unyielding, in spite of suffering, degradation, disease and the constant spectre of death.

While a student at the British Army Staff College, I met an officer who had been a prisoner of the Japanese. As he told his story, the savagery that had been inflicted upon him and his comrades was palpable, not just in his emotional and trembling voice, but also in his watery eyes, nearly half a century later. In recounting his experiences, he was a rarity. Few memoirs of the Chindit operations exist, and even fewer by the men who were captured. Survivors of the operations barely spoke about what they had done, even with those close to them.

Frank Berkovitch, in his short account of his time fighting with Wingate and his period in captivity, gives us a rare insight into the 1943 raid into Burma and the brutality of imprisonment at the hands of the Japanese. In Daniel Berke's quest to find out all he can about his grandfather's service with the Chindits and as a PoW, he has brought to life the stories of many others who served in this extraordinary unit. This book is a worthy tribute to those men. Reading it, no-one could have anything other than the utmost admiration for all of them, as well as gratitude for the sacrifices they made and the horrors they endured for the freedom we enjoy today.

Many of the men who fought in Burma, and particularly those who were captured, sustained mental as well as physical trauma which stayed with them for life and no doubt accounts for the silence of most of them. As a military commander I have witnessed the devastating effects that combat can have on the mental health of some of those who fight. There was little support for the Chindits and the many others who suffered in this way in the Second World War. Treatment and understanding have improved considerably in recent years, but the work of charities that support veterans remains extremely important as we continue to send men into battle. In honour of the memory of the fighting troops of the Chindits who carried the burden of their wartime experiences throughout their lives, the author is donating the royalties from the sale of this book to the charity Veterans in Action.

Colonel Richard Kemp CBE

Chapter One

'I've seen things you people wouldn't believe. Attack ships on fire off the shoulder of Orion. I watched C-beams glitter in the dark near the Tannhäuser Gate. All those moments will be lost in time, like tears in rain. Time to die.'

Blade Runner (1982)

We pulled into a car park in front of a modern, pre-fabricated building. I was in Bago, a town once known as Pegu, off the Pegu Road, near to Yangon, once known as Rangoon, in Burma. The building was a home for the elderly.

Seventy-two years earlier, at the end of April 1945, my grandfather had staggered along this road, along with 400 other men, prisoners of war, flanked by Japanese guards. The prisoners, barefoot, dressed in rags and loincloths, had suffered and witnessed indescribable savagery and were at the limits of their strength. They had nothing left but a will to keep going. Those who lost that will, who could no longer be supported by their comrades or persuaded to keep moving, were killed with a Japanese bullet or bayonet.

Also seventy-two years earlier, somewhere close to here, I cannot know where, the guards fled. Near to where I stood would be a village. A village called Waw. A village that is not on the map. A village where, seventy-two years earlier, my grandfather and the remaining survivors became free men.

Somewhere in a field near here, my grandfather and the survivors of the march out of Rangoon laid out a makeshift Union Jack to call for help.

Close to where I was, Allied planes thought they were Japanese and shot at them. Somewhere near where I stood, my grandfather clung to his friends as bullets raked up the ground. Somehow, near here, he dodged death again.

* * *

Had you walked past Frank Berkovitch during the later years of his life, the years I spent with him, you may have taken in his bow tie and trilby hat, for he never left home without them, nor did he walk past a lady without tipping his hat. As you passed him, you may have smiled at the portly, delightfully old-fashioned gentleman ambling by.

If, as he sat on a park bench, you were to have sat next to him and struck up a conversation, he would have spoken to you to exchange pleasantries but would not have offered any strong opinions. After you left and went about your day, he would soon have faded from your thoughts.

There would be nothing in his demeanour that would make you pause and wonder what was in his past. His movements were slow, nervous. His expression showed no hardness. There was sadness in his eyes and you may have sensed that he had known sorrow in his life, but nothing would have made you venture a guess that the man you were looking at was once a member of one of the most elite fighting forces in the Second World War, operating far behind enemy lines, deep inside some of the most inhospitable jungle on Earth. You would not have considered that here was a man who had survived two years of inhumane treatment and savage brutality at the hands of Japanese captors as a prisoner of war.

Some people want to talk. Some do not want to talk. I made a mistake with Frank, my paternal grandfather. I thought he did not want to talk. I knew he had fought in the Burmese theatre of war and that he had been a PoW, but I sensed that he did not want to open up. I was wrong. He did, but he just did not know how and so almost all I know was learned in the years following his death and, from what I know and as best I can, I will tell his story.

* * *

2

Frank was born on 5 August 1911 and was the son of Louis and Sarah Berkovitch, poor Jewish immigrants from Poland. After a rudimentary secular education, he studied as one of the first intake at the prestigious religious school, Gateshead Yeshiva. He spent his days learning the Torah and discussing its interpretations and commentaries in the Talmud. On leaving, he learned the trade of tailoring and, but for the Second World War, perhaps this would have been his lot: making suits, mending clothes and daily attendance at the synagogue. Then the world went syphilitic and his life, like so many others, took a drastic turn.

I was aware from an early age that he had been a soldier, had fought against the Japanese in the Second World War, and was a prisoner of war. I don't know how I became aware, I just was. Yet, until he died when I was 21, I knew very little about this time in his life. Over the years, I would pick up snippets from him and, despite the decades that have elapsed, I recall them with clarity; I knew he was a Chindit with Major General Orde Wingate, that he was a Bren-gunner and could strip and assemble a Bren in the dark in under a minute. He looked after the sick in Rangoon PoW camp and that in the camp they would give any eggs they managed to get to the sick men. I remember him standing in his lounge at home saying he was standing in the background in a field and a bullet whizzed by and nicked his thumb; he laughed when he said that.

He told us an anecdote about tracking elephants that he found amusing. Richard, my brother, told me that Frank said he had served as a batman (an orderly) to Wingate. Although I did not hear this, I do think it is likely for reasons which I will explain later.

I remember that he did not like me and my brothers playing with toy guns when we were kids; he told me it is a terrible thing to shoot a man. He was seated at the dining table in my parents' house when he said that and I don't think it is a hazy memory if I say he shook his head as he said it, as if he was trying to expel an image from his mind.

He was a quiet man, religious and serious. We would visit and play in the garden which backed onto a train line. We would watch steam trains go past, and each autumn he would climb a stepladder to reach into the branches of his apple tree and collect buckets full of apples which my mother would skilfully bake into pies.

As a child I did not find him great company; not bad company, just not very active or engaging. My other grandfather, Alec, was much more fun and became as much a friend as a grandfather. When, as a young boy, I asked him what he did in the war, I was slightly disappointed when he jokingly told me that he hid in a coal bunker; though that was partly true, he was, in fairness, a young teenager during the war years and too young to be conscripted. His wife, my grandmother Kitty, was a couple of years older than Alec. She told me that she drove a fire engine in the war. Manchester was firmly on the hit list of the German bombers. I didn't know she could drive.

'Oh I could, the men were away you see.'
'Sounds like you enjoyed it. I hope you weren't out dancing with American GIs!'
'I did not! And you know what we said about the girls that did!'

When I came home from university during the holidays, I would visit Frank at his small bedsit flat in the retirement home where he had lived alone in the years since my grandmother Millie had died. Among some trinkets, family photos and ornaments were his service medals. I would sit on his bed and he would sit in his chair next to his sewing machine and I would tell him about my studies as I worked towards qualifying as a lawyer, and I would ask if he was going on any day trips with other residents. So rarely would he ever volunteer anything from his past and somehow, I knew not to ask. On the few occasions that he mentioned the war, it was a short comment, which gave not even the slightest hint that this could lead to a conversation.

As he fell ill at the age of 88, I would visit him in hospital on most days. In the hours between visits he lay on his bed as his life drew to its conclusion, his mind still alert, thinking, remembering. Then one day I came home from having a drink with a friend after our lectures and it was too late.

He was a nervous man who did not like it if I did not drive slowly or, as children, if we were noisy. Looking back, he probably had Post Traumatic Stress Disorder or something similar. Probably his time as a PoW had damaged him; the horrors he would have seen and the constant fear must have eroded his nerve. I am angry with myself that I did not take the time to try to talk to him, though I question too whether it would have been right to bring up memories he had probably tried to bury for fifty years. He came home and, as best as he could, he shut it out.

*   *   *

In February 2015, on a flight to Vietnam, I open an old, tattered book which sat on my father's bookshelf, *Return Via Rangoon* by Philip Stibbe, and begin to read. Inscribed in the cover in my grandfather's spidery handwriting was a page reference and the words 'Frank's name'. It made me smile. Both he and Millie would routinely draw a cross over their own children in group photos and write their names on the reverse. They would look for a convenient place to put the 'x'.

It was the first time I had read a book about the Chindits: the special force created by Wingate to go behind Japanese lines and to fight them in the Burmese jungle. I had heard of the Chindits and knew my grandfather was in this force, and had heard of the famous Orde Wingate through the tales of his time in Mandate Palestine. I had no idea of what they did, suffered and faced. I had shied away from books about prisoners of the infamously cruel Japanese Imperial Army, knowing that once I allowed myself knowledge of their horrific crimes, I would be bound to imagine what my grandfather endured.

Philip Stibbe opens his account, written in the summer of 1945 just months after his release from captivity, with a powerful prologue which gives some insight into what the men of the Chindits faced. He found himself alone, far behind enemy lines to the east of the Irrawaddy River, wounded and without food, having been left by his comrades. These were the rules by which the Chindits fought. Each man understood that if he could not march, he must be left behind, at best with the hope that friendly Burmese would take care of them, though many were not friendly, or with a lesser hope that the Japanese would treat them well as prisoners, a rare occurrence. The reality though was that any men finding themselves in such a position would find their prospects, in Stibbe's words, 'extremely gloomy'.

Philip Stibbe was captured and followed a similar route of captivity to Frank. They were in prison together in a filthy jail in Bhamo, faced the sadistic guards in Maymyo and then were together in Rangoon Jail. In Stibbe's account of their time in Rangoon, there is a brief mention of Frank as the prison tailor:

> The clothing situation was little better. When we arrived we were all pretty ragged and most of us had nothing but the shirt and trousers that we stood up in. Soon the legs were cut off our trousers to provide patching material for the shorts that remained. The Japs produced a very limited supply of needles and cotton and one or two men, under Private Berkovitch, acted as tailors.

This was to be the first of several references to my grandfather that I would find. I can relate to it and it can make me smile. All the time I knew him he worked as a tailor. An old mechanical Singer sewing machine sat in his lounge. He would operate it by the pedal and deftly feed cloth through. At the Jewish festival of Purim, where children are clad in fancy dress and the Book of Esther is read, he would take orders from my brothers and I, 'I want to be Robin Hood', 'I want to be Dracula', and costumes would be stitched, a forest green suit with a quiver for arrows, a black suit with a red cape, and no idea or understanding that he had stitched the clothing of prisoners.

Yet this was not all he stitched in the prison camp. Other accounts of his needlework, read later in my research, left me fighting back tears and unable to sleep. Thinking about it as I write hurts. I defy anyone,

anyone, to do what he did with a needle and thread and not have their soul ripped apart by it.

Sometime later I found a document Frank had written, together with an extraordinary set of letters. It was in an expanding wallet of papers and my mother was having one of her routine clear-outs. 'Do you want this, or shall I give it to your brother?' I know I had seen this years before when I was a young teenager but don't recall reading it, or maybe I had and was too young or disinterested for it to mean much at the time. I took the papers. My brother already had two of the letters from the War Office which he had framed. One informed his mother that he was missing in action; the other brought her the news that he was alive and in the hands of the British Red Cross. What must she have felt on receiving that?

The document comprises thirteen pages of handwritten notes, written and signed by Frank. My father Tony thinks it was written for a student who was doing some research, an unknown student to whom Frank told more than he told his family. It became the basis for my journey to find Frank. It was his story. The tone, the choice of words, I can imagine him saying them. I can almost hear him saying them. Yet the story – his journey – I found hard to reconcile with the shy, pious man I knew.

It was his story. He was capable of telling it. He wanted to tell it. He wanted someone to listen. He wanted someone to ask. I was not asked and I had not asked. He told it to an unknown student. He did not tell it to us. Why? I had been selfish. I had not understood. I had not dared. I had not seen. He was scared. He was broken. He was shy. He did not know how to tell me and I had not told him that I wanted to know, that it was okay, that we could stop if it got too much.

Instead, I have just thirteen pages. The pages flow. There is no break, no change in writing style. He wrote this in one sitting, at his table next to his Singer sewing machine. He sat down and it poured out. Thirteen pages which could have been 130. Memories. Understanding. I tell myself that it would have dragged up the most heinous memories of a man taken to the edge of suffering, of lost friends. What right do

I have to bring this up? He buried it, like the friends he buried. Gone. Yet I know I am making excuses to myself. Buried maybe, but not forgotten, not gone, at least for him. He wrote it down, his words, his testimony, written with more passion, more feeling than I ever heard him express. He wanted to be heard.

His reticence to speak was common. Hardly any of the men who made it through the two Chindit expeditions – Operation LONGCLOTH in 1943 and Operation THURSDAY in 1944 – spoke about it to anyone, including their families. The mountaineer Joe Simpson made a documentary of his visit to Burma to visit the places where his father had fought in THURSDAY. His late father never once discussed it with him. He thought he had gone to Burma to say goodbye: 'It turned out I was saying hello.' My late Uncle Harry Weinmann served in THURSDAY, and his wife, my Aunt Joan, said that all he ever told her was 'I was small, but I was strong and fit.'

Sergeant Dickson's son Michael and grandson Richard sat in my house as I showed them the route he took as a member of 8 Column as he successfully evaded capture. He made it out to China and volunteered for Operation THURSDAY; he had never spoken of it.

Stephen Fogden, a leading researcher of the Chindits whose grandfather Arthur Howney served in LONGCLOTH and died in Rangoon, has collected numerous communications from families. A great-niece of one Chindit survivor wrote to Stephen: 'At Christmas, when he came to our house, he would speak a little and we remember him saying, after a few drinks, that the mules were the heroes in Burma.'[1]

Survivors of the PoW camps were told not to talk of what they endured as to do so would cause distress to the families of those who had died. Those who were not PoWs barely spoke either. There are a handful of contemporary books, mainly by officers. Scouring specialist bookstores and websites, each time I have found a book about the campaign, I have bought it and devoured it. When the books have been written by the men who served with Frank or their experiences quoted, I have read and re-read, and when Frank is mentioned in a line of text, or spoken of by an old comrade in an interview, or when I saw a snippet of film with him in it, it has been like finding treasure.

So without doubt, I am one of the more fortunate descendants of a Chindit because I have Frank's memoir. I read the precious words again and again. Thirteen pages. I read them so often that I know them by heart, word for word. Because we did not discuss it, I must imagine, and where I can rely on research and this precious memoir. I can imagine him looking after the sick as I saw how he devotedly nursed Millie (after whom my daughter is named) as she was dying from cancer. I can't imagine him lying prone, firing a Bren gun; I can't imagine him in hand-to-hand combat as he trained in India; I can't imagine him cutting through jungle. I can imagine him holding the hand of a dying man. I can see him whispering prayers. I can't see him holding a man down for a limb to be removed by a desperate doctor fighting to stop gangrene in a God-forsaken jail. I can see him bandaging the wound; I can see him pray. I can see him.

Frank served in the first Chindit expedition, Operation LONGCLOTH; a member of one of the toughest fighting forces of the Second World War, trained in guerrilla warfare behind enemy lines in the jungles as part of a pioneering 'long-range penetration' force. The lost army. The forgotten war. My lost grandfather. His forgotten memories.

He began his narrative with his own description of the Chindits and their aims:

Chindit, the name given to Orde Wingate's troops in the Burma Operations. The Chinthe is a mythical animal, half-lion and half a flying Griffin, it sits at the entrance to Burmese Pagodas to ward off evil spirits.

This authentic and moving recollection is of the high tension of the Wingate Expedition into Burma and behind Japanese lines in 1943. I remember and recall from my own knowledge, the magic of his influence and impact, which seemed to inspire the men.

He was a very striking and highly unorthodox character for the way he persuaded the War Office and the High Command to try what was called Long-Range Penetration into enemy territory and harass the enemy and cut their communications.

Chapter Two

'Like the generations of leaves, the lives of mortal men. Now the wind scatters the old leaves across the earth, now the living timber bursts with the new buds and spring comes round again. And so with men: as one generation comes to life, another dies away.'

Homer, *The Iliad*

Frank, like most of the men of his regiment, the 13th King's, was older than most front-line troops. Aged 27 when the war broke out, his initial posting was an easy one, based in England and assigned garrison and coastal defence duties. I can match the quiet, nervous grandfather I knew more easily to this posting than that of a hardened, trained jungle fighter. At a time when the seemingly invincible Wehrmacht was advancing through Europe, sweeping aside opposition, routing the British Expeditionary Force and causing their desperate evacuation from Dunkirk, it may be that some of the men of the 13th King's counted themselves lucky with their lot, though no doubt more than a few were frustrated and itching for action.

Frank, as a Jew, was attuned to the growing oppression of and attacks on Jews in Nazi-occupied Europe. Jews, as part of increasingly degrading measures, were required to wear yellow Stars of David. While the Nazis concealed their ultimate intention of murdering all the Jews in Europe, Frank's hands would have crushed the edges of the newspapers as he read the reports of Jews being herded into ghettos, taken away for forced labour and the attacks and humiliations in the streets. He would have read of *Kristallnacht* (the 'Night of Broken Glass', a pogrom against Jews). His community was involved in efforts to support Jewish refugees fleeing these monstrous events. It would have hurt to read these reports. It would have caused irrepressible anger; how could it not? Like all second-generation immigrants, he had relatives who had not left and were suffering under the evil of Nazism, the treachery of collaboration and the vileness of apathy. Hatred and anger would have raged inside him when he so much as heard the spiteful, false narrative of the Fascists. Had he been hoping to be sent to fight the Nazis? I suspect so.

Fate, as it so often does, had other plans. At the beginning of December 1941, the men of the 13th King's were told to pack their kit-bags and say goodbye to their families. Frank's father Louis may or may not have understood, or even been told, that his son was leaving to go to war. After the First World War, he had suffered a complete breakdown and was confined for the majority of the remainder of his life in a mental hospital. Frank told his mother Sarah that he was leaving. With no husband to support her, Frank did not want to add to her distress and so he told her not to worry, that he was not going to a dangerous part of the world. At this point he did not know, but best to not give her cause to worry, he reasoned.

With his kit packed and no idea of what lay ahead, on 8 December 1941, with the other men of the 13th King's, Frank boarded a ship bound for Africa, on his way to India.

The day before the men of the 13th King's set sail, just before 0800 hours on 7 December 1941, hundreds of Japanese Emperor Hirohito's pilots, having flown a short distance from the fleet of aircraft carriers with their escorting battleships, tore down out of the sky onto the unsuspecting and underprepared United States Fleet which lay anchored off Honolulu at Pearl Harbor. This was before a declaration of war by the Japanese which came the following day. In the attack, almost 2,500 US servicemen were killed and close to a quarter of the US fleet of 86 ships was damaged or destroyed. The US and Japan both declared war the following day, with Britain declaring war on Japan within a few hours. Three days later, on 11 December, Germany and Italy declared war on America.

The Imperial Japanese Army wasted no time, capturing Singapore without much of a fight and with it, taking 90,000 British, Indian and Australian soldiers captive. Malaya and Thailand fell quickly. The Japanese, fuelled by their *bushido* code, nationalism and an emperor to whom they had given the status almost of a deity, had also taken Bataan, Java and New Guinea.

During their occupation of these lands the atrocities they committed against natives and prisoners included enslavement, beatings, torture, starvation, rape, beheadings, medical experiments and cannibalism. Many such atrocities would be suffered by Frank and he could bear witness to them.

The advance through Burma was just as swift and the British defenders of Rangoon fled the city with the civilian remnants of the British Empire to begin their desperate escape march to India, harassed at every step by an enemy which was fanatical, determined and disciplined. In their retreat from Burma, the British Force was ordered by their commander Major General John Smyth to blow the Sittang Bridge. Smyth panicked, and in his bid to slow the Japanese advance, ordered the bridge to be blown when a significant number of soldiers and civilians were still on the east bank. Those who could tried to swim the river while under fire from Japanese troops. In no time the hard, fast fighting of the Japanese Imperial Army had galvanized their reputation as being the masters of the East, 'supermen' without equal in the jungle.

One of the most experienced generals in the British army took over command. General Archibald Wavell had fought in the Boer War, been injured in Ypres in the First World War, commanded forces in Egypt, Ethiopia, the Sudan and Libya and taken the surrender of more than 100,000 Italian troops before being replaced in Africa for failing to rout Rommel's Afrika Korps. He dismissed Major General Smyth immediately and appointed General Alexander (who commanded the retreat from Dunkirk) and the square-jawed, notoriously tough General Slim. Within a short period, they withdrew all British soldiers from Burma.

Wavell was not ready to give up so easily. He knew he needed intelligence from within Burma if there was to be a hope of fighting back. He also wanted to disrupt troop movements and communications. He needed an unorthodox officer and had just the man in mind. Orde Wingate had served under Wavell in various postings including Abyssinia, Ethiopia and Palestine. His methods of training regular forces to high standards and to operate as guerrillas against far greater numbers behind enemy lines had not gone unnoticed. Wavell sent a message from Delhi requesting Wingate's presence in Burma where he presented his view on how long-range penetration operations could change the course of the war. Wavell listened carefully and a short time later Wingate was told to travel to Maymyo, a colonial town in Burma, a place where my grandfather and other prisoners would later be beaten up and humiliated, and to put his plan into effect: to fight the Japanese, the masters of jungle warfare, far behind their front lines in the jungles of Burma, based on his belief that ordinary men, properly trained and led, could be developed into crack troops which could more than match the enemy.

No attempt to gain any insight of Frank during these years of war and capture can be made without some scrutiny of this enigmatic leader, a man described by Frank as a

man of powerful intellect, courage and determination…supremely self-confident, with ruthless and unorthodox ways and a very domineering element in his character and methods. But he could be very gentle in giving orders to his men as they harassed the enemy with their guerrilla attacks and penetration well behind the Jap lines.

As notorious for his refusal to conform, his untidiness and unwillingness to suffer fools as he was for his tenacity, intelligence and determination, Wingate was posted to the Sudan. He commanded native Sudanese and Egyptian men and gained first-hand experience of patrolling; not just as an effective way of hunting their quarry, but in training and developing soldiers, in navigating, working together and being alert. The seeds were planted which would grow into his unshakeable belief that ordinary men, with little or no experience of soldiery or combat, could be trained to be reliable soldiers, capable of fighting in hostile environments. It taught him something else too. It taught him to lead. I do not mean it taught him to give orders, but something more abstract and salient: to lead by example. To set the pace, to endure the same hardships as his charges and more, and to do so from the front. Wingate used his time in the Sudan developing as a soldier and testing his limits. Learning to navigate by stars in the wilderness, camping alone on the Blue Nile, hunting and foraging for his own food and taking long solo treks without food or water, developing his theories of guerrilla warfare that would one day be put into practice in the sweltering Burmese jungles.

Wingate arrived in Palestine in 1936. Palestine had been handed to Britain under a mandate in 1917 as the tide of war was turning. In the same year, Lord Balfour as Foreign Minister wrote his famed letter to Lord Rothschild announcing British support for the creation of a Jewish State in Palestine. His arrival followed two large waves of Jewish immigration from Russia and Poland between 1880 and the turn of the century and between 1904 and 1914, escaping State-sponsored pogroms and attracted to the idea of rebuilding the Jewish Homeland. Since Hitler's rise to power there had also been a steady influx of Jews escaping increased oppression, such as the Nuremburg Laws which placed severe restrictions on civil liberties for Jews and marked a major milestone in the Nazi programme of dehumanizing their victims.

For Wingate, arriving as a newly-appointed captain in the Intelligence Corps, there was plainly much to contend with. He had a striking face, clean-shaven at the time, with neatly-combed black hair, piercing blue eyes and a prominent jaw line. His trademark beard came later. His strict diet and self-imposed exercise regime gave him a fit physique.

Wingate, born into a deeply religious Plymouth Brethren family, had been brought up with the Bible. The names of Old and New

15

Testament places and the stories and events attached to them were well known to him. He became fond of quoting sections to his Jewish friends. As he walked through the underdeveloped land, the geography would have resonated deeply with him. As he walked the streets Jesus walked, he would have hiked the paths and hills where the battles of the Bible were fought, guided by the scriptures he knew so well.

Wingate had expressed strong sympathy with the Jews before arriving in Palestine. Once there, openly declaring himself a Zionist, he threw himself into learning Hebrew and became close friends with a number of leading Zionists, notably including the future first president of Israel, Professor Chaim Weizmann and his wife, with whom he and his young wife Lorna became very close. Years later, he and Frank would talk together, in India and Burma, late at night, when time allowed, as they bivouacked deep in the jungle and Frank, chosen by Wingate to be his batman, would ready his commander's kit and assist with carrying messages and orders.

The brigadier and the pious Yeshiva student discussed the stories and lessons of the Old Testament as they prepared to wage war. Perhaps, too, they spoke of the possibility of the establishment of a Jewish Homeland, which would come to be just five years later but which only one of them would live to see. 'I was convinced,' wrote Frank, 'he was a man of destiny, his missions into Palestine and Abyssinia and the successful infiltration of Burma had certainly shown this.'

Wingate may have told him about the land which was in so many of Frank's daily prayers and where Wingate, showing far more favour to the Jews than his brother officers considered appropriate, decided that the only way to challenge these attacks was by taking the fight to the enemy, using small, fast groups of British soldiers and Jewish men, trained to operate silently at night. The Jews under Wingate's command included the enigmatic Moshe Dayan who, in 1967, crushed the combined Egyptian, Jordanian and Syrian forces in just six days, despite being heavily outnumbered.

Wingate obtained the blessing of General Wavell, who was impressed with the plan and then worked to convince other military stakeholders.

The result was that he was given consent to form his Special Night Squads, small units consisting of about ten British soldiers and an equal number of Jewish fighters with a British officer. Wingate set up his HQ in Ein Harod, near Mount Gilboa, where in biblical times Gideon chose 300 men to fight the Midianites. Some years ago, I stood there and looked out at the same sweeping, sublime view of the Jezreel Valley that Wingate would have seen.

He taught the men how to plan raids and would sit with them to work out all the elements of cover, geography, placement of men and arms. Wingate had an unusual habit of sitting through such meetings naked, a practice he continued throughout his campaigns. The British and Jewish fighters naturally bonded through their shared hardships, successes and belonging to an elite band. They fought numerous engagements and carried out ambushes on unsuspecting Arab militants. At one battle, the largest they fought, near the Arab village of Dabburiya, Wingate was hit several times in the arms and legs in a friendly-fire incident. Despite his wounds, he continued to give orders before being evacuated to hospital. He was awarded his first Distinguished Service Order and made a full recovery. His squads lost just two of their own, one British and one Jewish. They accounted for about 12.5 per cent of Arab militant deaths.[1]

Emperor Haile Selassie, Lion of Judah, was in exile after the Italians had captured Ethiopia in 1935. In 1940 they were advancing on the Sudan, where the Allied forces were weak, small and vastly outnumbered by the Italians. Wavell, now in Khartoum, summoned Wingate to raise rebellion and reinstate the emperor.

Wingate, arriving in his scruffy uniform, lost no time in telling the staff that they had achieved little. With his firm belief in intelligence and research, Wingate was already well-read on the history of the campaign and the region and had taken several hazardous flights to learn the lie of the land. A pattern began to emerge in Wingate's development of his soldiers. In order to re-take Gojjam, he raised an armed force of local rebels under selected British officers, well-trained and small enough to move swiftly. It did not matter that they would be outnumbered: speed, surprise and tenacity would be preferred. He dismissed almost all the officers, considering them unfit for purpose. As he would with the Chindits, he preferred to take ordinary men, find the best of them and mould them into his vision. Creating a force around him he felt he could rely on, he named them 'Gideon Force'. Wingate was not fighting with numbers; he had instilled in his officers and NCOs the need to adopt guerrilla tactics if they were to win, using deception and ruses to confuse the enemy.

The tactics worked. While there were battles fought by the Gideon Force – bloody ones – it was by deception that Wingate was able to overcome the Italian forces. In one ruse, his men took the fort at the small city of Debre Markos and a war correspondent, fluent in Italian, used the still-functioning telephone to call each of the forts garrisoned by the Italians along the Blue Nile. Feigning panic, he claimed there was a huge enemy force closing in on them. The Italian garrison fled. A few years later, Frank would stand close by the bank of the Chindwin River, ready to cross into Burma with Wingate and the main Chindit force. Building on his experience, Wingate would start Operation LONGCLOTH with a ruse.

With the British forces having been pushed out of Burma, Wavell knew he needed to disrupt the Japanese and keep them from the Indian border. He was in need of an unorthodox commander skilled in training troops to a high standard, fighting in hostile environments, outnumbered and with minimal support. In Wingate, he felt he had the man he needed. So, on 27 February 1942, this flawed, enigmatic, yet highly capable guerrilla commander left England for India, and Frank, then in Secunderabad, India performing garrison and internal security duties, had no idea that his life was about to go through an enormous change.

Chapter Three

'Bushido is realized in the presence of death. This means choosing death whenever there is a choice between life and death. There is no other reasoning.'

Hagakure: The Book of the Samurai, Yamamoto Tsunetomo

During the war in Burma it is estimated that of 315,000 Japanese soldiers, almost 150,000 were killed in action or died of disease or suicide and more than 50,000 were wounded. Only 1,700 were taken captive and no officer above the rank of major.[1] The Japanese fought until they had nothing left. They fought to the death. They gave everything for their beliefs, and what anger I feel about their conduct in China and towards prisoners and to my grandfather does not detract from their extreme courage in battle. It was a courage born of fanaticism, nationalism and worship of their emperor.

As a fault of the arrogance of Imperialism, there had been a failure among the military and bureaucratic elite to learn about the Japanese culture, economy and ambitions. Many ignorantly dismissed them as an inferior race. That it was foolish to have done so is clear and the Allies paid for their arrogance and ignorance. The payment was made in blood and some of that blood was that of my grandfather's friends.

Japan had quietly modernized, purchased and manufactured weapons and expanded their sea, land and air forces. In 1937, Japanese expansion aims and tensions over the competing trade with China spilled over into a full-scale battle at Marco Polo Bridge. China was supported by Russia and the US, and Japan was not quiet in its threats towards the USA. By 1941, the threat was sufficient for Churchill to have said on 11 November that if Japan attacked the US, Britain would declare war on Japan 'within the hour'.

Attitudes towards the Japanese and their capabilities were swiftly rebutted. Two days after the attack on Pearl Harbor, two British warships were sunk off the coast of Singapore and Allied troops proved no match for the Japanese advance force as Singapore and Hong Kong fell soon after. Reports of the abilities of the Japanese soldiers as resourceful, tough and fearless fighting men quickly spread.

The nationalist military leadership held the Emperor Hirohito as a living god. Their code was rooted in the ancient samurai *bushido* code of morality and ethics, a code which held that war and death were a way to bring purity and that a warrior should be prepared and willing to die without fear. From a young age, Japanese children would learn of *bushido* and hear stories of sacrifice, death and honour.

For a soldier going to war, there could be no greater honour for him and his family than death on a battlefield. There could be no greater shame than surrender and capture. On 8 July 1943, Probational Officer Toshihiro Oura wrote in his diary: 'Father repeated in his letter that I must fight to the last as an honourable warrior. I will fight to the last, always for the emperor. I will show them that we will fight to the last.'[2]

For a low-ranking soldier, military life was harsh: beatings at the hands of superiors and humiliation were a daily occurrence. The elements of harsh training, scorn of weakness, a fierce warrior code given the status of a theological text, a living deity for an emperor, family honour and a large dose of peer pressure from officers and comrades all conspired to create a brutal, hardened force, enthused and pressured by a zealous belief in the war they had brought. This showed in battle and the approach of the Japanese soldiers to war. The Japanese infantry were taught to attack at night and advance without loading bullets in their rifles and to dull their bayonets by spreading mud on them to prevent the reflection of the moon or enemy gunfire. They charged into their enemy positions using bayonets as their main weapon.[3]

If it was typical to advance without bullets, there was a willingness to risk large losses of men for the sake of maintaining the element of surprise. A stray, early round fired might give away a surprise attack, yet rather than order the men not to fire, the standing order was to not even load weapons. Such an attack must therefore succeed by its stealth and the courage of the men who would charge with the bayonets or it would fail and the assailants would stand little chance against the hail of bullets that would be directed at them.

The enemy, or at least the British, were not an object of hate for the Japanese. Rather, an enemy which was in the way of their expansion but who also offered an opportunity for idealistic soldiers to test themselves against what they saw as an inferior culture and to show courage worthy of their *bushido* code, or to meet and accept death at the hands of a worthy foe. For those who allowed themselves to be captured by the Japanese, their treatment was appalling, being considered beneath contempt.

The war between China and Japan intensified and, if there were any doubts about the depths of inhumanity to which the invaders would go, these were dispelled in December that year, when troops of the Japanese army advanced from Shanghai and entered Nanjing in an orgy of violence. According to the Nanjing War Crimes Tribunal held in 1946, on the orders of Matsui Iwane, Commanding General of the Japanese Central China Front Army, in excess of 300,000 mostly unarmed Chinese were killed in a six-week period by first- and second-line Japanese troops. The atrocities included machine-gunning prisoners and civilians, executing prisoners and civilians with swords, with two officers holding a competition to be the first to behead 100 Chinese with their swords. There were acts of cannibalism by the Japanese and rape was widespread with women frequently murdered afterwards; children were not spared either.[4]

Japan used its advance into Burma in 1942 to cut off trade access between Burma and China. Yet a year later, small groups of Chindit fighters would escape Japanese patrols, through the jungle and mountains and into China to the safety of the Chinese General Chiang Kai-shek's forces.

China, Britain and the USA joined forces as allies to fight back against an army that was now known for its brutality, ferocity, discipline and courage. Wingate was tasked by Wavell with drawing up plans to fight the Japanese in Burma. Wingate took to the task with his usual attention to detail. He was a man who, unlike many, knew the importance of understanding terrain, gaining as much local knowledge as possible and of knowing his enemy. He needed to gain this knowledge quickly and, after making enquiries, he found the man he needed.

Mike Calvert was born to fight. By 1943, Calvert was a brigadier. By the end of his service he had been awarded the Distinguished Service Order with Bar. He fought throughout the world, in units which formed the seeds from which the British Special Forces grew and pioneered fighting behind enemy lines. He served as a Chindit commander and Wingate's key advisor in planning the raid. There can be no understanding of the Chindit operations without 'Mad Mike Calvert'.

He first saw service in Shanghai in 1937 and learned to speak Cantonese. As an 'observer' with the Chinese army, he was witness to huge, bloody battles with Japanese troops whose objective was the major port city. He wrote of seeing as much fighting in the few months of the fight for Shanghai between these two Asian forces as in the rest of the Second World War. He saw that the Imperial Army was growing in confidence and ambition and would inevitably turn its attention to land under British control. Calvert and his comrades gathered intelligence and submitted reports, but he was acutely aware that they were ignored. Notwithstanding the sheer negligence of the staff officers, Calvert maintained that what he learned in China stood him in good stead when he got to Burma. Unlike much of the officer class, Calvert respected the fighting abilities of the Japanese. He saw them in action at Shanghai and, after that, knew not to underestimate them: 'Too many men who did are now dead.'[5]

Attracted to danger, he joined the innocuously-named 5th Scots Guards, the alumni of which all moved on to Special Forces, including the 'Father' of the Special Air Service, David Stirling. In Norway he gained experience of blowing bridges on the Romsdal Gorge to slow the German advance, allowing him to put into practice demolition skills which he would use again to great effect in Burma.

Arguments for the need for Special Forces had started to be taken more seriously and found favour with Winston Churchill. Calvert attended a training course for guerrilla Commandos in Scotland, together with Stirling and a number of other like-minded soldiers. Calvert calculated that Special Forces, supported by air, could be deployed behind enemy front lines to destroy supply and communication lines and cause general mayhem. This was to be the role of the Chindits in Burma.

Calvert moved on to train in bushcraft in South Australia. He would take this knowledge and with Wingate would use it to devise a training programme for the Chindits, teaching them to read the ground, to identify potential ambush spots, to listen; to know that birds stopped singing when humans were nearby.

From Australia, he then moved on to Burma as the commanding officer of the Bush Warfare School in Maymyo, a pleasant hill town where, decades later, I walked around looking for the place where my grandfather was imprisoned and beaten. The Bush Warfare School was a front to train Chinese Commandos. Japan had not yet invaded Pearl Harbor, but Calvert saw a confrontation with Japan as inevitable and was in no doubt that Burma would be the key battleground. He was of course right and, as Rangoon fell, he took a group of men posing as Australians in their bush hats to try to trick the Japanese into thinking they were an advance party of a far larger force. Using hit-and-run tactics, they fought skirmishes along the Irrawaddy River, supported by a heavily-armed showboat he had pressed into service, before making his way back to Maymyo which was still in British hands.

His first meeting with Wingate came immediately after his return from his first expedition to Burma. Calvert was filthy and in a foul mood, but then Wingate began to ask questions about the 'showboat raid'. The questions were pertinent and Calvert began to pay attention.

His tiredness evaporated as they talked. Calvert had found the commander he could work with, and Wingate, the Grand Master, had found a key piece for his chessboard in Burma. Unbeknown to Frank, he was to become a pawn on that board and Calvert would make a profound and lasting impression on him:

Of the other men under his command, the nearest to Wingate in his views on the war in Burma was Major Mike Calvert. He had the talent for irregular warfare, for training guerrillas and commandos and the job of attacking the Japanese behind their own lines. Calvert was a natural rebel, but was full of ideas on irregular warfare; he had a great sense of humour and the wonderful zest for combat.

Wingate, with Calvert, now began to lay the plans to take the fight to the mighty Japanese, deep inside Burma.

Chapter Four

Thou, too, sail on, O Ship of State!
Sail on, O Union, strong and great!
Humanity with all its fears,
With all the hopes of future years,
Is hanging breathless on thy fate!
The Building of the Ship,
Henry Wadsworth Longfellow

The war diaries kept by Colonel Cooke and Lieutenant Colonel Robinson[1] were marked as 'Secret' and not to be opened until 2044. Fortunately, this was deemed to be longer than necessary and so I have copies. The diaries give some insight into the voyage to India and the training.

Lieutenant Colonel Robinson recorded that the men were taken from Blackburn to Liverpool where they were loaded onto HM Troopship *Oronsay*. He describes it as 'terribly overcrowded' and that 'arrangements were incredibly bad'.

Frank and the other troops, still ignorant of the purpose for which they were intended, sat cramped on the ship. The officers took the accommodation on the upper decks with the other ranks, including Frank as a lowly private, cramped and stuffy below decks. The steamer set off on 8 December and pushed out into the Irish Sea and then into the North Atlantic on a diversionary course with its cargo of 3,000 men. Lieutenant Colonel Robinson noted in his war diary:

9 December: 'joins convoy 30 troop and merchant ships, 11 warships – mostly destroyers. Weather very choppy.'

10 December: 'Gunfire heard – a destroyer rumoured to have opened fire on a submarine.'

11 December: 'more gunfire – this time at hostile aircraft. There was quite a storm during the night.'

21 December: 'with a Hudson flying overhead and in single file we steamed into the harbour of Freetown. We were immediately surrounded by "bum boats" selling fruit and they did a very thriving trade.'

I try to imagine what it must have been like. Staring up at a huge steam ship. Walking up the gangplank, laden with kit. The nervousness, the speculation, the confusion. Inside the ship, down below, jostling for space, arguing, joking. All soon giving way to boredom and frustration as the days rumbled on. Frank, who could never resist making a bet, would have joined in the card games, playing for small change and cigarettes in between their duties of keeping the ship tidy and daily exercises.

Frank had not been to sea before, nor had he left Britain. How was he on the journey? He does not mention this in his note, but there must have been some sense of fear. Allied ships were all a target for the German U-boats, the terrors of the seas. HMS *Barham* was sunk off the Egyptian coast just days before with the loss of 862 crewmen.

They left Freetown on Christmas Day 1941. Three days later Frank and the men took part in the ceremonial custom, famous among sailors: 'The Crossing of the Line', a high-spirited, alcohol-fuelled party in honour of Neptune as they crossed the Equator.

They landed safely in Durban and transferred to the RMS *Andes*. A later voyage did not fare so well when the *Oronsay* was sunk by an Italian submarine, the *Archimede* in October 1942, 500 miles west of Freetown with the loss of several crew members.

As the ship reached Durban and docked at the port, Frank and 3,000 men crowded the deck to be greeted by the voice of the South African soprano Perla Siedle Gibson, 'the Lady in White', who would serenade ships through a megaphone as they entered the harbour. Today a statue of her stands near the Ocean Terminal in Durban harbour. Durban was a pleasant three-day stop for the troops. Rationing was not in force and there was no need for a black-out each night. The men were made to feel welcome by the locals and had time to relax and visit the cinema, restaurants and bars.

After a false start, leaving on a ship which had to return to port, the men moved on to India, landing in Bombay and disembarking at the end of January 1942.

India? Tell me about India. A question to add to the list I didn't ask Frank. He could have spoken of the people, the garrison duties they did there, the military camp, the sights, the food. Yet I know nothing because I didn't ask. India in the twilight of the Empire. His memories, like ruined film, lost.

I chose to visit India and Burma. To say I followed in Frank's footsteps would be a gross exaggeration. My journey was little more than an attempt to see scenery upon which to project my images of Frank and his comrades as they prepared for the reality of war.

My father Tony had declined to join me a couple of years earlier when I travelled to Burma. He had thought carefully about it and I was very keen to persuade him. In the months before, I had been sharing the fruits of my research with him. He had called me. 'My Dad!' he said, after reading my notes, 'my Dad did this. Unbelievable. Never a word.' Yet he chose not to join me. It was my mother who explained; who told me that he didn't think he could go to the place where his father suffered so badly, and once she said that, I didn't ask again. India was different for my father. He did not worry that he would dwell too much on the suffering which was to come to Frank, and so he joined me in my modest pilgrimage. However, always there was that nagging feeling of how I wished I had sat with Frank and spoken with him of his time in India; how much more could I have taken to and from my journey.

My ever-wandering brother-in-law, an explorer and travel guide, described India as 'a story with a country. A story with many chapters.'

This story of the training in India of the men who would become the Chindits is just a short paragraph in the annals of an extraordinary country.

Today, we travel abroad loaded with information about our destinations: the customs, the scams; we share information on forums and download travel guides; we have high-definition colour films and documentaries. Frank and his comrades had a briefing from their officers. They were warned about how they should behave and, just as importantly, where they should avoid before moving on; strangers in a strange land. Frank walked the streets of colonial Bombay staring with wonder at the Eastern sights and vibrant colours: women in bright saris, holy men in white robes with painted faces. He was harassed by children and beggars and shouted at by vendors. He choked on the intense heat of local curry, so far removed from the blandness of the English food that he would not taste for another three years.

I have a photograph of Frank in India. He is about 30 years old and fit, with a chiselled jaw, sitting casually in his uniform with a cigarette. Dressed in khaki shorts and shirt with a pith helmet partially shading his face; self-confident, nonchalant, tough. The photograph was taken either in Durban or very shortly after the men arrived in Bombay. Another Jewish tailor in the first Chindit expedition was an EastEnder by the name of Leon Frank. He served as a member of 7 Column and was interviewed for a recording held at the Imperial War Museum. He said that in Bombay, the men swapped their pith helmets for bush hats. Leon's recording is an hour and a half long. He spoke of the training, fighting in Burma, his attempt to make it through to China. He shared his memories of his capture and imprisonment. It is hard to listen to. It was harder for him to speak. The torment in his voice is palpable as he recalled the horrors he endured and witnessed, as of course did Frank. However, right at the end of the recording he shared an anecdote, and it is about Frank and his bush hat:[2]

There was another fella called Berkovitch and he was a Jewish fellow and he was very, very religious. He used to pray every night; he was really sincere, like many of the lads with their own faiths. He used to sleep on his hat at night because we didn't have any pillows or anything like that, so he used to sleep on his hat on top of a block of wood. So when he put his hat on his head in the morning, he looked like Napoleon. He was the funniest thing out.

From Bombay, a sweltering, cramped twenty-eight-hour train journey took the troops to Secunderabad and it was from there that they were taken to the Saugor District of Madhya Pradesh, Central India for training.

Once the 13th Battalion, The King's Regiment arrived, they became part of the 77th Indian Infantry Brigade. This consisted of Gurkha Rifles, Mike Calvert's 142 Commando Company, the 2nd Burma Rifles (the Burrifs) consisting of local Karens, Kachins and Chins, eight RAF sections, a brigade section of the Royal Corp of Signals and a mule transport company. Together these men would form Wingate's Long-Range Penetration Force.

The force would be split into columns with a brigade headquarters' column to be commanded by Wingate. Each would consist of approximately 400 men and would be capable of operating independently of each other, though remaining in regular communication. Each column would contain a core infantry unit with a mortar team and Bren gun teams, experienced Commandos skilled in demolition. Local knowledge would come from the Burrifs. Animal transport officers would manage the load-bearing mules which were critical to the operation, able to transport heavy loads over long distances and harsh terrain.

Mules, as the saying goes, are stubborn. Handling them required patience, understanding and control. Not all the men were suited to this task; others such as Bill Smyly, a 19-year-old officer of the Gurkhas, was a natural and despite his youth was not afraid to chastise any man of any rank who mishandled the beasts.

Co-operation between the ground force and the RAF was a key factor in the success of the mission. The only way Wingate could see

29

the experiment succeeding was through re-supply by air. Men from the Royal Corps of Signals within each column would maintain communication between the columns and the RAF. Additionally, RAF officers were attached to each column to advise and coordinate the air support.

Frank wrote:

> We had a lecture from Wingate and every point was driven home in his own convincing way, about our commitments to take part in the recapture of Burma. Our job was to penetrate behind the enemy lines, to create havoc and to distract the Japs and cut all lines of communication. We would be supplied by air drops at designated sites (DSs).

Originally, there were to be eight columns plus Brigade Column, but 6 Column was disbanded during training due to a high failure rate, sickness and injury. The ones who made the grade were distributed among the other columns. The force was split into two groups. Northern Group, consisting of columns 3, 4, 5, 7, 8 and Brigade HQ contained 2,000 soldiers and 850 mules. The Southern Group, consisting of columns 1, 2 and a smaller Southern Group HQ, comprised 1,000 soldiers and 250 mules.

The force would have to fight more than the Japanese. The jungles, the rivers and the climate would all conspire to defeat men who were not fully trained and prepared. The topography was well suited to Wingate's needs. He had based his HQ at Jhansi where he had been training his officers and column commanders to lead the troops. As is traditional in the British army, the officers had a Mess where they would meet to discuss events and plans, as well as eat and have a drink together when they were not with the men. A cipher officer, Richard 'Willy' Wilding, joined after the training programme had begun. He wrote in his diary of meeting the officers of the brigade for the first time and noted that the 'Mess was run by a Pte Berkovitch – very efficiently.'[3] Nearby were the jungles of Abchand, Patharia and Orchha and the Sonar and Betwa rivers, where men could be trained in jungle-craft, river crossing and the techniques needed to keep them alive and to achieve their objectives.

Frank would be selected as a Bren-gunner and a member of the Brigade HQ Column. I remember Frank telling me he was a Bren-gunner, a weapon entrusted to those who had excelled in its use during training. The Bren was a light machine gun used by the British army from 1940 to 1992. Capable of firing 480 rounds per minute of .303in ammunition and highly accurate up to a mile, the targeted rounds of a single magazine could punch through a brick wall. Used properly, it could suppress an enemy and could be used to devastating effect in an ambush. However, it required skill and care in handling. To avoid jamming or overheating, typically it would be fired in short bursts of four or five rounds. It was designed to be fired with the operator lying prone on the ground or, with a firm stance, it could be fired from the hip. The weapon was critical for infantry soldiers in close-quarter jungle fighting.

All soldiers had some training in use of the Bren and extra ammunition was carried by men and on mules, so key was the weapon to each platoon. Together with the mortar teams and their explosive firepower, the Bren-gunners would cross rivers first in order to create and hold a beachhead, which could not so easily be achieved with small arms. Seventy-four years after Frank crossed the Irrawaddy, I crossed it with this thought in mind: that he was in one of the foremost boats, not knowing if he was in an enemy's sights.

On 2 June, Lieutenant Colonel Robinson wrote the following diary entry:

> … all last week and this week the Bn. has been on the range firing Brens and rifles up to 500 yards. The object has been to get A category shots to be able to kill the enemy at ranges up to 500 yards and B category up to 200 yards. So far the results obtained have not been unsatisfactory.

On 10 June Robinson wrote, with a note of pride: 'The Commanding Officer returned from GHQ [General Head-Quarters] this morning with the news that this Bn. has been selected out of the whole British Army in India to be trained as "Guerrillas".'

The training was extreme, punishing and as close to the conditions the men were to face as Wingate was able to make it. When they were not marching or on exercises, a training day would start at 0600 hours. They practised unarmed combat and bayonet training, learning how to close the last few yards in an aggressive charge, to stab and twist and move on, to parry and counter with the blades. This was all before they were allowed to have breakfast. They would then watch demonstrations and listen to talks in jungle craft and practise critical skills in map-reading, compass-reading and navigation.[4] By the time the training was complete, the men were experts in reading maps and terrain and could navigate by the stars to a very high standard.

Fighting is exhausting: the explosive forward moving force of punching, kicking, grappling and throwing. An unfit person will have less than a minute before their hands start to drop and they are gasping for air. The hand-to-hand fighting the Chindits were learning was never meant to last for even a minute. They were training to close with an opponent and beat them in seconds; look for the eyes, throat and groin, and use whatever was available as a weapon – a knife, a heavy branch, a stone – and keep attacking.

There was actually some opposition to this from some quarters. Major Fergusson, while proving to be among the toughest of jungle fighters and commanders, was from a far more privileged background than most of his men and carried an old-fashioned sense of propriety. The monocle-wearing Scot had served with Wingate in Mandate Palestine and had been impressed by Wingate's unorthodox methods. His friends had tried to talk him out of joining the expedition; career-damaging, hopeless and suicidal were among the arguments put to him.[5]

Fergusson denounced Kerr's fighting method as 'low-life gangster fighting', and he had a heated discussion on the subject with one of his men, a stoutly-built Welshman called John Kerr, later to be imprisoned with Frank, who wanted to teach the men. He argued that the Japanese soldiers learned ju-jitsu and the Chindits needed to know how to take them on if fighting went hand-to-hand.[6]

Ultimately, common sense seems to have prevailed over any old-fashioned British sense of fair play. The men learned to fight and to fight brutally. Wingate knew that fighting may be hand-to-hand. The men knew it and, for many of the men, the fighting skills they learned and the fitness they attained kept them alive when the time came.

Mike Calvert, already a hardened fighter, found himself in just this type of situation prior to the expedition when he had been carrying out reconnaissance. In an astonishing series of coincidences, his men had gone for a swim and he wandered off to bathe alone. A Japanese officer had done exactly the same and came across Calvert. Although he was armed and Calvert was already in the water, wearing only his boots (which he never took off outside camp), it seems that the officer heard British voices and decided not to fire. Calvert's group consisted of twelve men, but the Japanese officer could not know that and did not want to risk an open fight against an unknown number and risk his men's lives. Calvert knew he could call for his men, but did not know the Japanese strength. The Japanese officer, skilled in ju-jitsu, decided to fight Calvert hand-to-hand in the river. In silence, the men grappled in a fight to the death. Calvert eventually gained the upper hand and forced his opponent under the water, drowning him.

Calvert made it back to his men as the body of his opponent floated downstream. His men ambushed and wiped out the Japanese force of twenty men. He said of the incident that whether or not sensational press reports that he had single-handedly killed more Japanese than any other British or American soldier were true, on that afternoon, for the only time, he felt like a murderer and that many years later, the memory would come back clearly and all too often.[7]

And I wonder which memories came back to Frank, clearly and all too often.

* * *

Landing in Delhi, my father and I travelled by train about 250 miles south to Jhansi. My father had travelled to India thirty years earlier for business, but I had never been. We had chosen an enjoyable time to arrive as it was Holi, the Hindu festival of colour to welcome the spring. All those with whom I have discussed India talk about its assault on the senses and it is understandable; the tastes, colours, noises, smells and sights are all more pronounced. Frank did not pass through Delhi. His journey went through Bombay (now Mumbai) and both cities have changed enormously since he arrived in India, but cities are one thing and people and customs are another.

My first impression of India was hundreds of miles and decades apart from Frank's but he, like I, would have stared at the holy *sadhus*, returned the smiles of inquisitive children and gaped at the cows wandering along the roads and the horses adorned with religious decorations. Frank's train journey was twenty-eight hours and mine was an air-conditioned four and a half. Did he, like his son and I, stare through the window at the sprawling shanty towns outside the city and shake his head at the abject ubiquitous poverty, whether now or then? At the women in their brightly-coloured saris cutting crops with scythes and carts pulled by bullocks and mules, the wooden carts, heaped with sacks, pulled along by barefooted porters? Sights and sounds that will not have changed in the intervening years.

Jhansi is a dusty, grimy city of more than 1.5 million people, dominated by the fort where Wingate had headquartered himself to plan and to train his officers. The train station features briefly in the story of the Chindits and is busy, confusing and sweltering. As soon as we alighted, we found ourselves waving off the porters who had quickly surrounded us, and pushed through the mass of commuters, business people, families and beggars; for many, the station platforms were their homes.

Heading into Saugor, we came to a bridge over the Betwa. I stepped out from our car and walked along the bridge and then down the bank to the shore. The Betwa is one of two rivers on which the Chindits trained. Unlike the Sonar River, this one claimed none of the men's lives. The sun was up and the water glittered. It was blue and clear and beautiful. Somewhere near here, though I cannot know where, some of the men crossed over in a mock attack on Jhansi at the culmination of their training.

Much of the training was given over to long-range marches and night exercises, protecting bivouacs, river crossings, weapons training and mock battles. The men would march with full packs and weapons, accompanied by the mules that would pay such a vital part in the mission. In his memoir, Frank wrote: 'The Chindits infiltrated deep into Burma, laden down with a seventy-pound pack and Bren gun.'

The men wore standard issue clothing and were issued with 'Everest' aluminium-frame packs, though many stuck with the traditional unframed packs. They would all carry ration packs, a change of clothing, lightweight but warm Kashmiri blankets and bivouac kit, ropes for river crossing, water-wings which had been designed for the mission, rubber-soled hockey boots, cooking kits and water. Each man was issued with silver rupees. Wingate insisted that all food and services from Burmese civilians be paid for; winning hearts and minds would make it safer for any future Allied expedition to rely on local support and would reduce the danger of betrayal. This contrasted with the Japanese approach of, at best, paying with worthless paper money and at worst simply taking what they wanted, often accompanied by violence. The brigadier also made clear that no man was to behave improperly towards Burmese women, stating that were this to happen he would personally shoot the transgressor in front of the offended locals.

All men would carry 4 hand grenades and 4 magazines for the ammo-hungry Brens, in addition to 100 rounds each for their own rifles. Each platoon was issued with grenade-launcher rifles. All men carried bladed weapons: the Gurkhas would carry their traditional kukri, a long curved knife, with most of the others being issued with a *dah* (rather like a machete); vital tools to cut through jungle and to build rafts as well as for hand-to-hand combat. Many of the men also carried flick-knives acquired in Bombay as an 'ace in the hole'. As ammunition was used up, it would be replenished by air. One man even joked to his officer that they should sharpen the teeth of the mules so they could fight.

Some 70lb (or 32 kilos) plus a Bren gun, another 21.5lb (or 10 kilos): a total of more than 90lb; half the body weight of an average man. Frank and his comrades would march hundreds of miles bearing this weight in some of the most hostile territory in the world.

Any parade drills were immediately dispensed with by Wingate; he had no time or patience for traditions and was the last man to concern himself with tidiness and shiny boots. Saluting was more or less stopped and the men were told to dress comfortably. If they wanted to roll up their sleeves or march with their shirt open, that was fine, as long as their weapons and kit were kept in good order and they could march and fight. One officer wore a kilt, another had a pair of .45 pistols slung round his waist like a cowboy[8] and Wingate himself was often the most curiously dressed – or undressed – of all, occasionally seen naked but for his boots and his pith helmet with an alarm clock round his neck, while munching a raw onion. When he did wear clothes, he dressed as the men did, with no insignia to mark him out as the brigadier.

The monsoon rains that fell in Madhya Pradesh during June and July created landslides, flooding and extremely muddy conditions. More lives were lost in training due to the extreme weather conditions than in weapons-related accidents.

The jungles in which they trained in India were different to the jungles of Burma. The jungle in Burma is far thicker; at points barely any light penetrates the canopy and visibility is measured in feet and inches. There is simply no standard type of jungle. A jungle is an area of uncultivated, thick-growing forest in a tropical or sub-tropical area. There are no constants and the type of vegetation and density will depend on a wide range of factors. In thick jungle, navigation becomes extremely difficult. Natural landmarks such as mountains are out of sight and the stars are also hidden from view.

The men needed to learn, during this training period, all they could about survival in such an alien environment; how to deal with leeches, which bugs, roots and leaves could be eaten and which were poisonous, how to stay safe from snakes and when to kill and prepare a snake to eat, how to make camp, to find trails and, perhaps above all, to source water.

The jungle, for Frank and for so many of the men, must have seemed daunting. The forests of Abchand and of Burma are teeming with wildlife; from birds and fowl to monkeys, deer, tigers and wildcats. Also some nastier surprises: vipers, cobras, spiders, rats and all manner of creepy-crawlies, right through to buffalo and elephants, many of which were used as beasts of burden. In a way, it was an elephant that may have saved Frank's life, but that is for later in his story.

Of his initiation in the jungle, Frank wrote in his memoir: 'Memories of my first night in the jungle were not good ones. No sleep was possible, with the noise of the shrieking birds and rustling in the undergrowth, all sounds alien to a city boy.'

Pulling off a highway, we parked at the top of a valley from which we could hike down into the Abchand jungle. Immediately on leaving the car, a monkey sauntered into my view: he had come quite close and then leaped onto a rock from where he studied us for a moment before losing interest and deftly climbing a tree. From our vantage point, the trees stretched out like a carpet of green. In a month or so, the leaves of the native trees would become deep red and yellow, earning them the name 'Flame of the Forest'. Growing among them were banyans and gum trees. The footpath faded into a rocky descent down a gradual cliff into the valley and the small stones increased in size to larger granite rocks and boulders which we clambered down, becoming enveloped by the trees as we went.

Reaching the bottom of the valley, we were rewarded with a view into the jungle to which superlatives will do no justice. On either side of the valley the rocks rose steeply, with the Gadheri River cutting through. The sides of the valley were thick with trees that arched inwards, creating a channel going deep into the forest. Light burst through the trees and glittered on the water. Monkeys were running along the ground and through the rocks and their chattering to each other from the trees mixed with the calls of birds high in the canopy. A slice of untouched paradise and as far from the grimy, industrial streets of 1940s' Manchester as could be.

I stood with my father, looking out over the river as it disappeared between the trees. It was stunning, mesmerizing. The ground was tough: rocks and boulders and vegetation. We had gone but a short distance. To march through this for miles with packs and weapons would have taken effort and perseverance. To me, but almost to himself, my father said: 'Imagine going all the way through this. My little Dad.'

Descending, the granite rock became steeper and I continued alone without my father, jumping from boulder to boulder and at some points using hands and feet to climb down short sections. The rock was an orange hue and as we moved downwards, the trees began to thicken again. I traversed along a small path to a space beneath a large stretch of rock which jutted out, just around head-height. Ancient paintings adorned the rock face, some in red, some in red and white. Two animals fighting, an elephant with men on it, an animal being hunted and a group of soldiers, with their weapons, marching to a battle, just as Frank, passing through the same land, would do centuries later. As I marvelled at the paintings, an owl swept over me and perched on the rock face; the perfect hunter.

We moved on to the foot of the valley. The steep rock faces of the valley had fewer trees and the sun beat down on the Gadheri as it flowed between the cliffs. I do not know whether the men passed through here in training. The jungles are large and were far larger in 1942 before much of it was cut down to make way for development. Perhaps they waded through the valley and marched over these rocks. If they did not, they would have marched through similar terrain. We were there during the Indian summer; the men of the 77th trained during the monsoon. The rocks would have been slippery, the rivers fast-flowing and deeper, the nights longer.

Whatever fear Frank and his comrades felt of the jungle, Wingate refused to tolerate it. Men armed with modern weapons and human intellect should have no fear of any animal; he determined that the Chindits were to see themselves as the apex predators in the jungle.

Gradually, the 77th became used to the jungle. The animals avoided the men and the sounds and sights became sufficiently familiar that the men were soon walking through it as easily and comfortably as if they were going for a walk in the countryside.

Robinson recorded in his war diary: 'The training is getting on quite satisfactorily and the men are beginning to find the jungle is not quite such an awe-inspiring thing in the dark as they first thought. Everybody still has a very healthy respect for the snakes.'

Surrounded by thick jungle and with the Betwa flowing through it, Orchha is an ancient city with palaces rising high above the trees. The palaces of Orchha, built in the sixteenth and seventeenth centuries, are the palaces from which Rudyard Kipling took his inspiration for the palaces of *The Jungle Book*. The men trained in the teak jungle around Orchha, practising their bushcraft techniques, their drills in choosing and protecting bivouac sites, always away from tracks, in the cover of jungle, with listening and sentry posts. Animals had to be unloaded and no bivouac could be settled into unless the men all had full water bottles. They trained to 'stand to' before dawn, ready with eyes scanning the trees for any unusual movement, and then moving off again with packs and weapons for another day of training.[9]

There was no downtime during training. Breaks from marching and weapons practice were spent on map-reading and jungle craft, but eventually, as they passed into Orchha they were given a couple of days to relax. The men explored the Raja Mahal where *sadhus* sit in meditation and the Lakshmi Temple with its fresco paintings of the famed Rani of Jhansi and her battle against the British, of royal hunts and Hindu gods. They walked through the Jahangir Mahal with its mix of Hindu and Muslim architecture, topped with ribbed domes and upturned lotuses. Elephants are carved into the stone over the arches and narrow walkways. From the outer balcony they looked out over the seemingly endless carpet of green teak trees of the jungle through which they had trekked in the days and weeks before.

As we walked alongside the palaces that the Chindits explored, I saw a parrot perched alone in a tree, a bright green parrot with a red beak. It is forbidden within the Jewish faith to tattoo the skin. A curiosity of Frank's was that he had tattoos, almost unheard of among observant, orthodox Jews. One of these was a parrot on his forearm. As a kid, I asked him about this. He told me he had it done in the army. I pointed to the parrot and remarked to my father that it reminded me of his tattoo. He agreed; another of Frank's paradoxes. I certainly do not wish to romanticize the jungle. No doubt for the most part it was fearsome and testing, but I believe that Frank was able to find an affection for it and his tattoo was proof of this.

We walked through the Orchha jungle. We had reached it over an eighteenth-century bridge. The water was rocky and clear and a number of locals were washing and swimming in it. As we entered into the forest, which stretches all the way to Rajasthan, we looked back through the trees and over the river and could see the domes of the palaces high above the city.

The forest was dense, mainly teak trees and 'Flame of the Forest', but also rhododendrons and Kharadi trees which only grow in the sub-tropical climates of India and South America. The ground was littered with granite rocks and rock pools and small ponds had formed, each home to numerous species of insects, amphibians and fish. We could hear birds above us and everywhere, we could see and hear monkeys, always close but at a respectable distance.

During the monsoons, much of the forest along the banks would be flooded as the river widened and quickened.

As we were there, a convoy of lorries arrived containing spotted deer. They were there in abundance in the 1940s and were being reintroduced, as are leopards, to keep up the population. I looked over at my dad as he looked around him in wonderment, walking through the same jungle that his father had walked in seventy-five years earlier.

* * *

High levels of sickness became a problem; some genuine, others not. Certainly the climate, mosquito-transmitted diseases, jungle sores and training injuries were a serious problem. On 13 August Robinson recorded 'another man died of dysentery', but as morale dipped through sickness, Wingate was on hand to lift spirits. Frank commented on Wingate's communication skills in his memoir: 'The moment Wingate got up to speak he did not have to search for words.' On 6 September, he spoke to the men. Robinson recorded his impression of the brigadier's address:

> The Brigade Commander addressed the whole Battalion for about an hour in the most masterly fashion. The general opinion was that he put more heart into the Battalion by his speech than anything else that has happened for a long time. The whole standard of the Bn, the health, the morale are going up perceptibly. Hardening, toughening marches etc. are being done every day and the number of sick is rapidly decreasing.

Wingate pressed his officers harder than his men. Each one had to learn 800 words of Urdu and were consistently to report on progress of training: whether non-swimmers could now swim, whether the muleteers were coming along as planned, whether signals had been taught. He would creep up on officers he saw without their weapons to show how easily they could be taken unawares and unarmed. His alarm clock hanging around his neck was used as a constant reminder that time was against them.

Marching was a key component of training and helpful not just to toughen up the men and establish a high level of battalion fitness, but also to weed out those who were not up to the task. Men were not forced to keep up or shouted at or threatened; if they chose to drop out then they were left to find their way back to camp and that was the end of their involvement in the Wingate expedition. Hundreds dropped out, unable to bear the weight of the packs, the distances of marching and the deprivations, their nerves shredded from live firing exercises and grenade and mortar practice, knowing always that there was worse to come.

Frank stayed the course. Each time a man gave up and dropped out, he resisted the temptation to follow. As he crawled into his makeshift shelter known as a *basha* at the end of a night march, he fought down the voice that told him to stay there and not continue. His body became conditioned as his capacity for exercise increased and his muscles developed; he became accustomed to the weights and the distances, skilled with weapons, and with these abilities his self-confidence grew as, day by day, the tailor became a soldier.

It was at some point, in India, that Frank became Wingate's batman. This was one of the few memories he did share with family. Not the detail, simply the fact that he was given this role and, with pride, that Wingate had chosen him. As a batman, his role would be to carry messages, assist in running orders to officers, and maintain the officer's kit (presumably this was an easier job with the notoriously untidy Wingate who eschewed shiny boots and brass). In combat, a batman was expected to stay close to his officer to run messages and, if needed, to act as a bodyguard.

I have a photograph, possibly a cutting from an article in a magazine. Front and centre is Wingate, rifle in one hand, sporting a safari jacket and his trademark pith helmet. He is smiling, with his bright, intense eyes looking straight at the lens. He is flanked by men in equally scruffy uniforms, with bush hats, all smiling and at ease. At Wingate's right shoulder stands Frank. Unlike the other men, he is looking at Wingate rather than the camera. Under his arm is a sheaf of papers: orders, plans, records and information.

Wingate understood the importance of the press. He appreciated that he was a maverick and many of the officer class were against him. He was often willing to give press conferences and to speak to journalists. Some video footage was taken of the Chindits as plans were laid for the raid into Burma. It was all embargoed until after the expedition. Judging by the healthy condition of Wingate and the men in the footage, this was before they crossed the Chindwin on

13 February 1943. Standing right next to the brigadier, smiling and wearing a comically oversized bush hat and looking just like my father in his younger days, and perhaps quite like me, was Frank.[10]

* * *

The columns trained to march in snake formation, with a column of 400 men strung along in single file with more than a kilometre between the front and end of the column, rather than the typical 'three abreast' formation in which British soldiers typically marched. This was not simply because the tracks in the jungle, insofar as they existed, were too narrow, but because it also allowed the best response to ambushes and sudden engagements. If the column was attacked then far fewer men would be caught in it than if they were bunched and marching alongside each other. The column could break off with the men quickly slipping into the jungle in groups to meet at a prearranged rendezvous, or they could choose to outflank and encircle a small attacking force. Again and again they practised breaking off, taking positions, dispersing and firing.

The officers would train with the men. Wingate believed in leading by example and expected it of his officers. They would eat and sleep with their men and each officer would carry the same pack weight, with additional kit such as binoculars, a revolver and a rifle or Sten gun. They would march on foot rather than on horseback. At the time this was rare in the British army, but the men of the ordinary ranks were impressed to see that as they marched, all officers from the brigadier downwards joined them in marching on foot.[11]

The men were fuelled by army biscuits. Notoriously tough, they would joke that they could be used for armour-plating. The biscuits were supplemented by tinned meat rations and by whatever they were able to hunt; peacock was popular as was game and goat, even some unfortunate monkeys found themselves on the menu. They were also provided with a huge stock of onions which the brigadier insisted be eaten for their supposed health-giving properties. A rare question

I asked Frank, who in the years I knew him observed a strict diet according to his religious traditions, was whether he managed to keep kosher at all, avoiding meat in favour of other rations. He told me it wasn't possible as even if he did not eat meat, the food was cooked in non-kosher fat and once he was in the jungle, they ate whatever they could. It was no breach of his faith though. Jewish doctrine makes clear that dietary rules must be broken in favour of sustaining life when there is no other option.

The training diary records that on 13 September a lengthy marching exercise began with 120 miles of marching in five days with full kit, personnel and animals. They marched 16 miles across country 'ending up with a very cold night outside Balabahat', followed by mock attacks and practice road-blocks over the next two days around Saugor. Marching continued over the following months with a 24-mile march on 7 December and a 22-mile march across country on 10 December and another 20 miles on the following day. Then, on 12 December, a 23-mile night march to Larwari. By this time, many of the weaker men had already been weeded out and spirits began to increase as the men came to enjoy the lengthy marches and sense of achievement. By this time the men and their officers were capable of marching at an impressive 4 miles per hour.

On 15 December, the force left their bivouacs and, following an 8-mile march, carried out another mock attack on a bridge. Using mortars, they practised capturing the bridge, which was defended by two platoons, before sending in sabotage squads to blow it up. British military training typically had one-sided battles, with the enemy simply being a series of flags. Wingate and Calvert saw no sense in this. All the mock battles were fought with blank ammunition, in as close to real conditions as possible. Frank, with his Bren on his shoulder and his 'No. 2' feeding him ammunition from a belt or from magazines, directed blank rounds towards the opposing force. After the battle they then marched a further 8 miles to Burdwan in three hours during the night.

On the Betwa River, near a railway bridge, Wingate ordered all columns to take part in full river crossings, as columns, with mules and rafts. They were to keep essential kit like radios dry and to test the rubber water-wings to assist the men to stay afloat. After a first practice, expected to take several hours, they would carry out a further practice as part of a mock attack, securing a beachhead under fire. Further training at the Sonar River went badly during the monsoon rains while the river was raging. Three men from the ill-fated 6 Column lost their grip on a rope and were swept to their deaths. The waters broke the banks and a number of Gurkhas had to be rescued by their comrades using inflatable rafts held with ropes to prevent them floating away. Others who could not be reached found themselves spending the night high up in branches of the trees.

While in Saugor, we arranged to meet a local historian, Dr Rajnish Jain of Saugor University, and a journalist, Abishek Akash, who had reported on a story about the Chindits. We met in the Circuit House, an old colonial building from 1893, next to the military cantonment. Sitting on sofas draped with white lace beneath a portrait of Mahatma Gandhi, we listened to Abishek tell us of an article he had written about a brigade of Indian soldiers of the 31st Armed Division who, a year earlier in February 2019, had marched close to 400 kilometres through jungle as a recreation of the Chindit training marches, going from Babina near Jhansi to Dongargaon. The Indian soldiers used the trek to connect with indigenous tribes inhabiting the region and to organize medical camps for their benefit.

Dr Jain suggested we may want to see the English Garrison Church and so, with him in our car and Abishek leading the way on his Royal Enfield motorcycle, we set off to the large, imposing building, painted in white with a red roof and three white spires. The gate was locked so I followed Abishek over the wall. A young girl came from a small hut within the grounds. Dr Jain explained that we would like to look inside and she returned with a key and her younger brother to open up. As we walked over, Abishek asked me what rank my grandfather had attained in the army. 'Was he a senior officer?' he asked. 'Just a private,'

I said. 'Is that an officer?' 'No,' I replied, 'just a plain soldier.' Later, over a very spicy lunch of *dosas* at the university café, Abishek asked if I had a photograph of Frank. I sent him a copy of my photograph of Frank in India.

The church had a surprise in store for us. The inside was much like any typical Anglican church: pews, stained glass, altar and decorations were all as they would be in England. On the walls were gilded plaques and memorials to army officers and church members and their families who had died or given their generous support. We had expected little from the church, save as a reminder that one chapter in the story of India was that it became part of the British Empire.

One footnote to that chapter was recorded on the wall of the church. Among the plaques was one made conspicuous by its simplicity: a grey slate with white text. I walked to it and the names, names I recognized, jumped out at me. The plaque reads as follows:

Lt. Neville Nathan Saffer
C.S.M. George Bateman
Sgt. John Hill
L/Cpl. Herbert Owen Bell
Pte. Francis Donald McKibben
Pte. Harold Marsh
Pte. Glyn Jones
Pte. George Parker
Pte. Ronald Braithwaite
Pte. George Turtle
Pte. Henry B. Savage

All Members of the 13th Bn. The King's Regiment.
They died on active service during the last half of 1942 while the Regiment was stationed in the neighbourhood of Saugor.

'There's some corner of a foreign field that is forever England.'

Neville Saffer from Leeds – like me, he was a Jewish solicitor with a passion for boxing – was killed by a negligent discharge aged 33. George Bateman, Harold Marsh and Francis McKibben were swept away and drowned in the swollen Sonar River. Ronald Braithwaite was a Commando who died of injuries sustained during an explosion during training. The other men all died of disease.

'Mr Tony,' Dr Jain asked my father, 'What does this mean, there is some corner…'

'It means wherever they are buried, they were serving England and so they lie in English soil. Wherever in the world, wherever they died.'

The memorial, stark and clinical, stands as a testament to the harsh training in unforgiving conditions.

In the late afternoon, we walked through the Patharia forest, a further region where the men had trained, where Frank had fired his Bren, learned navigation and survival and marched mile after mile. The forest is now 500 acres, less than half the size it was in 1942. Much of it was cut down to make way for housing and for the university. The forest is carefully managed and walking trails have been set down, so rather than climbing over rocks and through trees as we had in Abchand, we simply took a pleasant stroll along the trail for a few kilometres. The forest around us was thick with bamboo, teak and jackfruit trees and as we walked we could hear the calls and songs of birds. The forest is inhabited by house crows, songbirds, sparrowhawks, owls and Indian grey hornbills; just some of the species of birds. Butterflies and dragonflies were in flight around us. The forest once had Asiatic lions and panthers and these would have been there when my grandfather was here, but they had since died out due to deforestation, hunting and conflict with humans. There were still plenty of snakes – vipers, cobras and, growing up to 22ft in length, pythons – all kept in check by the local snake-catcher.

The following morning we met our guide Hermant for breakfast. He was grinning widely and brandishing a copy of a daily newspaper. It was the *Dainik Bhaskar*, a national Hindi newspaper. Splashed across the top of the inside cover was a picture of me looking at British graves near to the garrison church, which had fallen into ruin, together with a picture of me and my father in conversation and my picture of Frank. The article told of our journey to the region to see where Frank and the Chindits had trained and spoke of the mission into Burma. My dad was delighted to see that the article referred to Frank as a British officer. He said his dad would be very pleased with the promotion and we shouldn't correct it.

* * *

As 1942 came to an end, Wingate wrote an order for his officers titled 'Maxims for all Officers', the very points he wanted to be impressed on the men. The maxims give an insight into the nature of the tactics he knew were needed for the mission to succeed:

Secret
(29 Dec. 1942).
77th Indian Infantry Brigade
Maxims for all Officers

1. The Chindwin is your Jordan, once crossed there is no re-crossing. The exit from Burma is via Rangoon.
2. Success in operations depends on the perfecting of an exact and well-conducted drill for every procedure.
3. Our reply to noise is silence.
4. When in doubt do not fire.
5. Never await the enemy's blow, evade it.
6. Fight when surprise has been gained. When surprise is lost at the outset, break off the action and come again.
7. Security is gained by intelligence, good dispersal procedure and counterattack. Thus all depends on good 'guerrilla'

procedure plus careful drill. Read and then re-read 'Security in bivouac'.

8. Always maintain a margin of strength for a time of need. It is the reserve of energy that saves from disaster; that gives the weight required for victory.

9. Avoid defiles. If you must use them, secure your flanks first. Pass by night whenever possible. For us, a defile may be defined as a track from which dispersal is not possible owing to physical obstacles.

10. Times of darkness, of rain, mist and storm, these are our times of achievement.

11. Never retrace your steps.

12. The movement of the column must be unpredictable, even for its own members.

13. Never bivouac within three miles of a motor road or waterway. Three miles of good forest will give the same protection as ten miles of open country.

14. Use your W/T (radio) to capacity; it is your greatest weapon.

15. Use every weapon and every man to capacity. It is their combined and simultaneous employment that gives strength. Work together and rest together.

16. *Festina lente* (make haste slowly). Let your haste be a considered haste, the fitting end to a leisurely examination and preparation. Speed should be the result, not of fear and confusion, but of superior knowledge, planning and drill.

17. Intelligence is useless unless it is passed on. Use your W/T.

18. See that your men think the same of the situation as you do. For this, constant talks and explanations will be necessary.

19. Get rid of casualties; never keep serious cases with the Column.

20. Spend your cash.

Signed Orde C. Wingate (Brigadier Commander 77 Ind. Inf. Brigade).

At the end of the Saugor exercise, the final mock battle took place. The objective was the capture of Jhansi railway station, 120 miles to the north.

The Fort of Jhansi is a formidable structure. Built by a Bundela chief in 1613, it has a commanding view of the city and is surrounded by several thick granite walls, with high ramparts, cannon emplacements, firing slits and accessible via a sturdy, imposing iron gate at the end of a single, steep path. It is famous among Indians as the place from where Lakshmi Bai, the Rani of Jhansi, defied the British during the Indian Mutiny after refusing to cede control of her city.

The British stormed the fort when the garrison refused to surrender. The Rani, with moments to spare, grabbed her young son, jumped on her horse and, followed by her bodyguards, leaped from the walls and escaped east to Gwalior. Joined by other rebels, she led an assault on the Fort of Gwalior and captured it, before moving on to engage the British at Morar, where she was killed in the thick of the battle. Wingate, who made a point of learning local legends and history, would have heard this story and thought of the Rani with the respect due from one rebellious soul to another.

The men were marching day and night, under the weight of full 'Everest' packs, accompanied by the mules that bore the weight of 3in mortars, extra ammunition, radios and the heavy batteries. At the end of the march, all columns took part in the battle to capture Jhansi. The columns fanned out and a force feigned an attack with a feint from the east, but the attack was to come from the west. Platoons in the attacking force were ordered to attack via a bridge over the Betwa, roadblocks were set and the saboteurs carried out demolitions. I do not know which side Frank was on. The attacking force came under heavy fire from blank rounds, but their speed was enough to sweep through the defences and lay an ambush for a counterattack. Under as realistic conditions as could be, the battle was successful, with the men operating at full fitness, following orders and displaying initiative.

Wingate had taken men, previously average men mainly in their late twenties and early thirties, and brought those who had shown the willingness and ability to complete the training to very high levels of fitness. They were now highly skilled with rifles, bayonets, explosives, versed in jungle-craft, river crossings, working with mules and laying ambushes. Yet this was not enough. The logistics, communications, rations and plans had to be carefully prepared. Wingate had ensured that by placing RAF officers with the columns, as well as signallers and radio-operators, communication could be maintained, as best allowed by conditions, between the Brigade HQ column and the other columns and between the ground force and the RAF who would drop supplies of ammunition and rations at prearranged drop sites.

This had never been done before and large amounts of time were spent in planning and preparing for this undertaking. The planning paid off. Throughout the expedition, RAF pilots, with nothing more than a map reference and a natural feature to go by, made repeated drops with pinpoint accuracy.

Rations were a major problem for Wingate. The men would face the exhausting tasks of cutting through jungle, crossing rivers and patrolling many miles of the most challenging jungle and mountainous terrain. Rations were needed that would provide 3,000 calories per day, to be supplemented with food that was either caught or bought from locals. The ration packs contained the high-fat and energy army biscuits, nuts, raisins, cheese, chocolate, sugar and tea. The calculations were wrong. The distances to be covered, the weight carried and the speeds with which the Chindits needed to move were such that they would burn calories at a high rate. Often villages were far from each other, or may be occupied by the enemy and need to be avoided. A village may not have enough food spare from their subsistence lifestyles to sell to a column. Likewise, hunting and trapping take time and patience and while food may be caught, it was likely to be only enough for a few men, not several hundred. By the end of the mission, none of the columns had received their full allotment of rations in the field. On average, they only received half and consequently all the men who made it out of Burma came out seriously malnourished.

A further problem to be considered was what to do if men, far behind enemy lines, could not march with their column due to illness or injury. The options were all atrocious, but every man understood. It would take all the reserves of each man to operate in the jungle and achieve their objectives. They would be outnumbered, they would need to fight and march and move quickly. An injured man who could not march would slow down and risk the entire column. All men had received basic first-aid training. If possible, the wounded could be taken to a village in the hope that it would be a friendly village that would take care of the wounded. If there was no friendly village nearby, the wounded could be left with a gun, water and rations and advised to surrender to any passing Japanese patrol as they would stand at least a small chance of survival. At least one Chindit in this situation turned his gun on himself; there may have been more among the many who would be reported as 'missing in action'. The officers were also supplied with morphia and had been taught how to administer, if necessary, a lethal dose.[12]

Wingate needed to decide what to call his force. This was a matter of some debate among the officers, but was settled after Wingate had been walking alone around Jhansi. He spoke with a Burmese holy man and asked about the statues of the beasts at the entrances of the pagodas. Half-lion, half-eagle, to Wingate they represented the co-operation needed between his land force and the air force. The beast is called the Chinthe, and was altered slightly to Chindit. Frank also explained in his memoir the meaning of the word: 'Chindit, the name given to Orde Wingate's troops in the Burma operations. The Chinthe is a mythical animal, half-lion and half a flying Griffin, it sits at the entrance to Burmese pagodas to ward off evil spirits.'

By the time training was complete, Colonel Cooke had little doubt about the ability of the Chindits. He wrote in his war diary: 'We are now probably amongst the highest trained, fittest Bns [battalions] in the British Army, about to embark on what will probably be the most exciting task ever performed by a British Bn.'

What of Frank? I think he enjoyed India. I believe he loved it. Why? Because he did not drop out as many did. He made the grade. He pushed himself; he carried his 70lb of kit over every mile, every inch of Indian soil that was asked of him. He was entrusted with the critical fighting role of a Bren-gunner with his platoon. From the man who described himself as a 'city boy', he became a soldier in perhaps the most exotic place on Earth, among ancient forts, in jungles and, alongside the other men who had stayed the course, ready to take on whatever was to be thrown at him.

The training complete, the men marched along the Manipur Road at night reaching Imphal, close to the eastern border of India. Passing through Imphal and Kohima, the Chindits saw the desolation and remains of the destruction of the retreat the year before: derelict trucks, skeletons and discarded belongings.[13] Two and a half years later, British and Indian soldiers would force the Japanese from Imphal and Kohima in a battle that raged for three months. A monument stands sentinel over the rows of Commonwealth graves at Kohima, bearing the now famous epitaph:

'When you go home, tell them of us and say,
For your tomorrow, we gave our today.'

As the men arrived in Imphal, on the border with Burma, Wingate addressed the men. He warned them that anyone who fell behind would need to be left. Once they crossed over that was it and there could be no turning back. He urged anyone who did not feel up to it to step forward and leave the unit. Maybe, like others, Frank felt doubt. They would be going to war, outnumbered by at least ten to one, behind enemy lines, in the jungle, with limited support and the knowledge that if they couldn't march, they would be left behind. Maybe it crossed his mind to step out of line. He didn't. Nobody did. They were in this now, together. The 'jossers' who had failed to make the grade had been weeded out. No man, having completed the gruelling training, chose to withdraw. The time had come for the Chindits to cross the Chindwin and go to war.

Even at this stage, it was not clear that the mission would go ahead. A Chinese offensive into Burma had been called off and Field Marshal Wavell (as he now was) had to decide whether or not the Chindit raid should go ahead, despite there being no follow-up offensive by a large force. Wingate persuaded Wavell to support the initiative on the basis that they would gather valuable intelligence on Japanese forces and gain experience of fighting behind enemy lines in the jungle. Calvert described Wavell's decision, in the face of much opposition, as 'courageous'.[14]

The men were paraded for Wavell, himself no stranger to courage having won the Military Cross and lost an eye in battle in 1915. Whatever effect Wavell had on the men, as they stood ready to make a final march from Imphal in India to Tamu in Burma, across the hills separating the two lands and on to the Chindwin River, the men had a greater effect on Wavell. In an action possibly unprecedented in military history, as the men marched off, Wavell, out of respect for the extraordinary mission before them, saluted the men before they saluted him.[15]

Chapter Five

Cannon to right of them,
Cannon to left of them,
Cannon in front of them
Volleyed and thundered;
Storm'd at with shot and shell,
Boldly they rode and well,
Into the jaws of Death,
Into the mouth of hell
Rode the six hundred.

The Charge of the Light Brigade,
Lord Alfred Tennyson

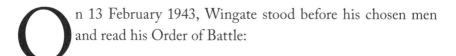

On 13 February 1943, Wingate stood before his chosen men and read his Order of Battle:

Today we stand on the threshold of battle. The time of preparation is over, and we are moving on the enemy to prove ourselves and our methods. At this moment we stand beside the soldiers of the United Nations in the front-line trenches throughout the world. It is always a minority that occupies the front line. It is still a smaller minority that accepts with a good heart tasks like this that we have chosen to carry out. We need not, therefore, as we go forward into the conflict, suspect ourselves of selfish or interested motives. We have all had opportunity of withdrawing and we are here because we have chosen to be here; that is, we have chosen to bear the burden and heat of the day. Men who make this choice are above the average in courage. We need therefore have no fear for the staunchness and guts of our comrades.

The motive which had led each and all of us to devote ourselves to what lies ahead cannot conceivably have been a bad motive. Comfort and security are not sacrificed voluntarily for the sake of others by ill-disposed people. Our motive, therefore, may be taken to be the desire to serve our day and generation in the way that seems nearest to our hand. The battle is not always to the strong nor the race to the swift. Victory in war cannot be counted upon, but what can be counted upon is that we shall go forward determined to do what we can to bring this war to the end which we believe best for our friends and comrades in arms, without boastfulness or forgetting our duty, resolved to do the right so far as we can see the right.

Our aim is to make possible a government of the world in which all men can live at peace and with equal opportunity of service.

Finally, knowing the vanity of man's effort and the confusion of his purpose, let us pray that God may accept our services and direct our endeavours, so that when we shall have done all we shall see the fruit of our labours and be satisfied.

Wingate's words had a powerful effect on the men. Stirred by their commander's zeal, they left feeling proud and determined. Frank does not say how he felt about this speech, but he does talk about the effect Wingate had on him:

The moment Wingate got up to speak he did not have to search for words. He knew exactly what to say about the great possibilities of this type of warfare, of long-range columns of men behind enemy lines. If ever a man had risen to an occasion, it was Wingate; there is no doubt that Wingate was a man of powerful intellect, courage and determination.

Yet of this land, this almost mythical land, part of my history where my grandfather gave so much, where he left so much behind, in the jungles, the battles, the camps, I knew nothing of Burma. Tonmakeng, Tatlwin, Pinbon, Nankan: all distant places. Places where Frank had marched, fought, sabotaged, blown up bridges or a railway. Twinnge, where he was ambushed and captured; Nampaung where he was thrown in a cage; Bhamo, Maymyo; names of places of his suffering, places I cursed without having seen.

In a specialist travel bookstore, I bought a map of Burma. There seemed to be an abundance of maps of other countries and regions but only one for Burma. I put some of the names into Google Earth. Some were there, others not. I could not find Nankan or Tatlwin; I found Baw, which from the images seemed to be no more than a field. I found Inywa, Tonmakeng and Bonchaung. I was conscious that spellings transliterated from a different script may be different and tried various formulations but simply could not find some of the places named. Twinnge looked to be a small village shrouded in trees next to the muddy river; it did not even appear on my paper map. From the grainy satellite image it was so tiny. For Frank, at the moment of the ambush, it was his entire world as his life hung in the balance.

Although crude, the officers' maps from the expedition provided some assistance. As the British had been in occupation for some time before the Japanese invasion, there had been plenty of information from traders, local knowledge which would doubtless have proven of assistance in creating military maps. The maps did show names of villages, and forests, rivers and high ground are clearly marked. It was fairly clear that the land was populated with small village settlements and plenty of mountainous land and jungle.

Burma is a confused land, largely cut off and isolated. Its golden age began in the eleventh century when King Anawrahta unified the land into a single state, centred at Bagan, under the Theravada Buddhist faith. For 1,000 years at least before this, traders travelled the routes between India and China, the gateways between which passed through Burmese land; a fact not lost on the Japanese centuries later.

Dynasties rise and dynasties fall and Burma was no different. After expanding too far, Burma found itself in conflict with the

British Empire, which effectively took control of Burma and made it a province of India. There was a strong resistance campaign to which the Empire responded with severity. One of the rebels who was executed by the British in a public beheading was Bo Min Yaung. His grandson Aung San and great-granddaughter, the controversial Aung San Suu Kyi, would go on to be the most celebrated and revered of modern Burmese leaders.

It is no surprise then that Aung San, an active student leader, took a nationalist and fiercely anti-British stance. In seeking support for his cause, he met Japanese military officials who easily persuaded him to go to Japan. With his like-minded small band of co-revolutionaries he formed a group dramatically named the 'Thirty Comrades' and, with a blood oath and taking *noms de guerre*, they received military and tactical training in Japan, as well as arms and finance. These young men, with Aung San as the leader, would go on to form the pro-Japanese Burmese Defence Army.

The importance of geography in this conflict cannot be underestimated; in a land of 675,000 square kilometres, the landscape, borders, climate, obstacles and populations all had their parts to play.

Burma is bordered by China to the north and north-east, Laos to the east, Thailand to the south-east, Bangladesh to the west and India to the north-west. To the south are two bodies of water: the Andaman Sea and the Bay of Bengal. It has roughly the shape of an upside-down electric guitar and is just shy of 1,000 kilometres at its widest part and double that in length. The heights of the country are in the north, where a range of mountains reach as high as 5,881 metres (Mount Hkakabo). Many of the peaks are extremely steep with sheer rock faces. The peaks are the sources of the rivers flowing through the land. The lowest points are the Irrawaddy and Sittang river deltas, both of which feature in Frank's journey.

The terrain was, and is, tough; tough enough to have put off many commanders, though not Wingate. To cross from India into Burma, the Chindits would need to cross the imposing Arakan Yoma Range, stretching down from the staggering heights of Tibet into Northern

Burma. The mountains in this range, though small by the standards of the Tibetan mountains to the north, were still formidable, dwarfing anything within the British Isles. The smaller peaks are around 500 metres higher than Ben Nevis's 1,345 metres and the higher peaks more than double its height.

Burma is within the Asian monsoon region and has three seasons: it is dry from late October to mid-February, then hot and dry from mid-February to May, with monsoon rains from the end of May to mid-October. The monsoons were a constant threat to the Chindits. There was a window within which to operate. If they were not out by the time the monsoons arrived, the rivers would become deadly torrents and impassable barriers.

More than half of Burma, even today, is covered in rain forest. Depending on the location, soils, height and rainfall, the vegetation consists of huge mangrove trees around the Irrawaddy, with vast areas taken up by razor-sharp elephant grass standing 8ft high. The Chindits had to battle through the grass, hacking with *dahs* and kukris, each man taking the lead for a few minutes before dropping back for the next man to take over. There are forests thick with rhododendron and oak trees in the north and through the areas of the country where there is less rainfall, and large hardwood forests containing valuable teak; sadly, the prized nature of teak for furniture has become its curse. When I was travelling north from Mandalay to Katha, our vehicle became stuck behind a convoy of trucks, snaking along roads as far as I could see, all laden with teak trunks and bound for China.

Dissecting Burma and the lives of the Chindits, like scalpels, are two major rivers: the Chindwin and the Irrawaddy. The Chindwin, 1,200 kilometres in length, is a tributary of the Irrawaddy. It flows into Burma from the northern mountain area in the Kachin State and meets the Irrawaddy to the south of Mandalay. The Irrawaddy, dubbed 'The Road to Mandalay' by Rudyard Kipling, is the main commercial river within Burma. Originating from the Mali and N'Mai rivers in the north, it cuts through the length of the country, draining into the Andaman Sea to the south. It is sacred to the Burmese: the river of spirits. It provides their daily water needs and their transport; it provides income for fishermen and connects villages. It almost dries in summer but, swollen by the monsoon, it is fast-flowing and dangerous. I have sat in a sampan boat with my hands in the water. It is cold and the flow is strong and pulled so strongly that the boatman had to press the wooden boat into the current so as not to veer downstream as we crossed.

For Frank and the Chindits it was the greatest of obstacles. Relentless, implacable and ever present. Wide and open and with no way around. The ruthless, chilling waters ready to sap whatever energy and will a man had left. Add into the mix the machine guns and mortars of the enemy dotting its shores and the Irrawaddy was a terrific, terrible foe.

As important to the expedition as the geography were the inhabitants and, of course, the enemy.

The ethnicity of Myanmar is very diverse. The main ethnic group is the Burmans, accounting for 70 per cent of the population, followed by the Shan. There are Mon, Chin, Rohingya and numerous other groups. Significantly there are groups of Kachin and Karen Christians who played a major role in helping many of the Chindits in their journeys out of Burma.

Some 90 per cent of the population of Burma was, and is, Buddhist. There is a sizable Christian population, mainly within the Kachin, Chin and Karen groups. Each Buddhist I asked about the Christian minority assured me they are treated as equals, though the Christians with whom I spoke said that this was not the case, feeling that they suffered discrimination. This ran deep and had been the case long before the current administration. It was this sense of bias that had partly fuelled a desire for independence among the Christian ethnic groups and, during the Japanese occupation, led many to at least sympathize with and often actively assist and even fight alongside the British.

For many of the Chindits who broke out of Burma, going north into China, help came as they were nursed, fed and passed from village to village by Kachin hill tribes.

The many ethnic groups break into smaller groups: for example, the Chin comprises more than fifty ethnic groups and the Kachin twelve. So there are hundreds of different groups, numerous languages and many faiths. Even today, only 30 per cent of the population lives in towns and cities, with the majority living in villages. Many of the villages will not have changed since Frank's time, based on farming crops and livestock, with houses made of bamboo and wood on stilts to avoid flooding during the monsoon seasons. The villagers live with several generations under each roof and villages work together communally. Throw into the mix the poor roads and transport and isolated inhabitants, and the result is a population with no cohesive aims, limited communications and an insular mentality. For a soldier separated from his column or a small dispersal group of men trying to escape back to British lines, it meant that if you had to approach a village or a Burmese local, it was a gamble and the stakes were life or death.

Buddhism underpins daily life for the majority of the population, and the landscape in inhabited areas is adorned with pagodas, *stupas* (shrines) and statues of the Buddha in positions of teaching and rest adorn the land.

On early-morning walks I would be met with the sight of monks, from child novices to adults, barefoot and shaven-headed wearing simple robes and carrying rounded black bowls with lids in which locals would place alms of rice, curry, vegetables and meat. Women were at markets with their faces painted with the white thanaka paste worn as a decorative protection from the sun. Villages would have pagodas at which prayers are offered and where gold leaf and gifts of food and incense could be placed on the Buddha. I watched religious processions, I saw devotees and monks prostrated before statues, and I heard the mesmerizing sound of monks chanting their incantations; sights and sounds just as seen by Frank seventy-four years earlier. It is the unchanging nature of faith and tradition, passed down from generation to generation. It was into this ancient, confused land that the men crossed to carry out their orders in Operation LONGCLOTH.

* * *

Wingate started with a ruse. As the men readied to cross the Chindwin River, Wingate's 'Jordan', he sent two columns, consisting of almost 1,000 men, led by Majors Dunlop and Emmett under the command of Lieutenant Colonel Alexander to travel further south. Their objective was to draw the Japanese away from the main body of troops. This southern group, nicknamed 'Decoy Force', would draw attention to themselves by cutting the railway south of Wuntho.

The main force, dubbed 'the Killing Force' by Wingate, would cross further north. The plan was for the Decoy Force to deliberately draw attention to themselves and thus reduce the number of Japanese troops in the area of the main Chindit force. This would mean the larger northern group would have more time and space to destroy railway lines in the north without significant opposition. If all went well, Wingate would then have the option to press further east across the Irrawaddy River.

The southern group crossed the Chindwin River at Auktang. Further north, the main body of 2,000 men crossed the Chindwin at Tonhe. The crossing was not easy. The Chindwin is fast-flowing and wide and the men had to handle inflatable boats, equipment, infuriating mules and help each other across. Once across, both groups faced the fiercest jungle: thick bamboo, razor-sharp elephant grass and creepers hanging down from the canopy of trees that blocked out the sky. They hacked through. Often it was impassable and they had to re-route and find a new path or wade through streams. As they reached their bivouac, before they could strip and burn off the parasitic leeches that had attached themselves to the sweat-drenched soldiers, before they could make tea or cook a meal, they had to secure the perimeter, sort out their kit and clean their weapons. The ATOs would unload, rub down and feed the animals and the signallers would prepare the large wireless sets to contact brigade. Only then could they take a rest.[1]

As they passed through the dense jungle into the more open teak forest, the southern group made every effort to be spotted. Taking a large air drop that could not be missed, they then marched to a village known from intelligence to have pro-Japanese sympathies, and occupied the village, making a pretence of setting up a temporary HQ. One officer, Major Jeffries, was dressed in the uniform of a brigadier, the logic being that the Burmese would describe the insignia to the Japanese who would believe that this was the force commander. Plans were discussed loudly and villagers were 'carelessly' engaged in conversation with Burrifs and plied with misleading information about numbers and plans. However, the deception worked and the Japanese, drawn to the reported goings-on further south, were nowhere to be seen.

Frank's memoir is fairly scant on his time in the Burmese jungle. He makes no mention of crossing the Chindwin and just briefly summarized some of the places they passed through, actions they took and battles they fought before the force was ordered to return to India, many of them having marched close to 1,000 miles: 'The Chindits infiltrated deep into Burma, laden down with a seventy-pound pack and Bren gun and fighting many actions along the way.'

After Colonel Alexander's feint had been allowed time to work, drawing the attention of the Japanese from the main crossing, the southern columns moved off to cut the Mandalay-Myitkyina railway lines near Mandalay, carrying out numerous ambushes on unsuspecting and often careless Japanese patrols on the way.

Marching from Tamu, the northern columns marched into the dense jungle to cross the 47 miles to the Chindwin River. Passing along elephant tracks and the occasional motor road, Frank and the Chindits would have seen the bodies of soldiers and civilians who died or were killed in bombings and attacks in the desperate retreat from Burma.

Frank had been issued with a small grey *Prayer Book for Jewish Members of HM Forces*, from which he would recite his daily prayers. It contained prayers that are not in the usual prayer books found in synagogues and Jewish homes. Written in Hebrew script and with English translations, there was a prayer for the wounded, a prayer for going overseas and a prayer for battle:

Unto thee, Heavenly Father, I lift up my heart in this hour of trial and danger.... Give me the strength to do my duty this day as a true and loyal Israelite in this War for Freedom and Righteousness. Fill me with the faith and courage of those who put their trust in thine everlasting mercy; and lead us through victory unto peace.

With this prayer on his lips, during the night of 14 February Frank, with the brigade column as part of the northern group, crossed the Chindwin unopposed. The crossing was slow, in small boats. The light machine-gunners, probably including Frank, crossed over first and fitted their weapons to anti-aircraft mounts to protect the rest of the force from any air attack as it crossed. Crossing with the force were bullocks, mules, elephants (one of whom was swept away with a large amount of kit) and the faithful column dogs. The dogs were local strays that had been trained to run messages in boxes tied to their necks between platoons. At least one of the dogs named Judy survived the whole expedition, and alongside her dispersal group eventually crossed back over the Chindwin River to British lines.

The land on the eastern bank was sparsely vegetated and open, with little cover. The men needed to cover it quickly. Even if there were no Japanese troops in the area, news could still reach them quickly. The Chindits needed to move fast to get to the cover of the jungle and to the site of their first air drop. Frank hoisted his pack and weapon and they set off at full marching pace. They covered a staggering 36 miles in thirteen hours; a distance and speed which simply would have been impossible but for the rigorous training they had endured.

As Frank noted, they collected supplies after an air drop the following day at Myene. It went smoothly, with the RAF working with pinpoint accuracy and timing. After the supply drop the columns split off to meet their objectives, heading towards the east.

Wingate aimed to cut the vital Mandalay-Myitkyina line at various points, as well as blowing bridges, harassing enemy patrols and destroying anything of use to the Japanese. The railway line had to be reached on foot through dense jungle, mountains and over *chaungs* (streams), and the passes between the jungle villages were riddled with Japanese patrols.

Frank moved out with Wingate and his column. The brigade column served a different function to the other columns. As well as being able to function as a fighting force, it worked as the executive branch from where major decisions were made and as the central force through which intelligence and reports of engagements, objectives and movements were received from the other column commanders.

After seven days' marching over mountainous land, they reached Tonmakeng where there was a further successful air drop. The frequency and success of these air drops were vital to keeping the troops re-supplied with ammunition, medical supplies, kit and food. The RAF would drop into the landing strip, marked out by fires, from a low height of about 70ft, throwing out several packages per run, each plane carrying out eight or nine runs. One of the men who flew on the air drops was Major Wavell, the son of Field Marshal Wavell.

As an aside, courage clearly passed from father to son. Major Wavell, MC served in the second Chindit campaign in 1944, where he lost a hand in battle against the Japanese. In 1953, he died in battle when his twenty-strong Black Watch platoon was surrounded by Mau Mau rebels.

Frank wrote: 'After we collected a successful air drop we then marched hard and moved forward to attack a Jap Garrison at Pinbon. We blew bridges behind us, then through the village of Tatlwin and on to Nankan where we blew up the railway and then we crossed the Irrawaddy.'

Their march to Pinbon was a distance of about 100 miles as the crow flies from where they had crossed from India into Burma, through the hills of the Mu Valley before they dropped into the valley and crossed small tributary rivers. Pinbon is one of the places in Burma that I was unable to visit. The political situation and the poor infrastructure and transport links limited much of my travel. Aung San Suu Kyi and her National League for Democracy held some power, but it remained a power-sharing government and the military remain ever-present and powerful. Chinese influence is strong, with large companies controlling significant tracts of land: areas where jade and rubies were mined or where teak was logged were off limits. Roads were poor between major towns and often little more than tracks between villages and, during rainy seasons, whole areas are cut off.

If anyone in the brigade column kept a diary, it has not been published and despite a lot of searching I have not been able to find any books or accounts, so other than Frank's brief comment, I have no record to describe the attack on the garrison. The best information I have is recorded in the report of the debriefing of Wingate.[2] The report reads: 'Finding Pinbon and neighbourhood strongly held and patrolled by the Japanese, Wingate ordered No. 4 Column to ambush the Mansi motor road and seek to by-pass Pinbon through the mountains.'

There is no mention of the attack Frank was in; however, it is likely that this would have been one of the smaller actions in the vicinity. West of the Irrawaddy, Wingate was less keen to avoid confrontation, and as an early part of the mission was actively keen to 'blood' his troops: to show them that whatever had been reported about Japanese soldiers, if they were hit by a bullet, they went down like anyone else. The detail of what happened I will never know, apart from his brief comment 'We then marched hard and moved forward to attack a Jap Garrison at Pinbon.' I know that somewhere near there, Frank lay prone; the powerful recoil of the Bren thumping into his shoulder in what may have been his first taste of combat.

As the Japanese forces at Pinbon were attacked, Fergusson's 5 Column and Calvert's 3 Column slipped further into Burma: Calvert to blow the railway and Fergusson to blow the bridge at Bonchaung. Frank, with the brigade column, set off before the enemy had a chance to pin them down. Setting out on 2 March, they marched in a large force down the Pinbon-Pinlebu motor road. Wingate set up roadblocks and had the bridges blown behind them. Although Frank wrote 'We blew bridges behind us', it is very unlikely that he took part in the demolitions. The report records this being done by 7 Column and it is likely that the charges were laid by the Commandos who formed part of each column and were trained in demolitions. It is far more likely that Frank used 'we' to describe the force he was with as a whole. The rain was heavy at the time; not monsoon rain but sufficiently heavy to make the road impassable for motor transport. Frank trudged on, the mud sapping his energy, and bivouacked in the forest about 10 miles north-east of Pinlebu.

Learning from Calvert that the Kaingmakan route to Wuntho was clear, Wingate moved with the main body of troops towards Wuntho. No. 4 Column, however, was unable to join. On 4 March, battle was joined with a much larger Japanese force near Nyaungwan. In the course of the battle, the radio was destroyed and much of the equipment was lost. The Column Commander Major Bromhead made a decision to march his column back to the Chindwin River and cross back into India.

No. 2 Column ran into serious difficulty. On 2 March, an officer made a mistake in allowing his 250 troops to march along a branch railway line in broad daylight; a serious error of judgement that went against Wingate's tutelage to avoid tracks wherever possible. The officer took this route as the quickest way to reach the main line. Inevitably, though, the Japanese became aware and sent an infantry company of about 180 men. The column bivouacked near the main line and then broke camp at 2130 hours, after darkness had fallen, to commence demolitions. As they filed out, they were ambushed. The Japanese light machine guns and mortars immediately took out a number of men and mules as the rest of the men dived for cover. The ensuing battle was brutal. The Japanese opening salvo was answered rapidly by the British Bren guns, spaced along the column. Small arms were fired at each other and then the Japanese, with typical mettle, charged the British line. Chindits and Gurkhas hurled grenades as the Japanese infantrymen came within throwing distance but still they came, through the shrapnel and the bullets from the British Tommy guns, and the battle went hand-to-hand, bayonet-to-bayonet.

The column broke into dispersal groups and they ran into the jungle, dodging fire from the Japanese troops who were in pursuit, with some of the groups in further hand-to-hand fighting as they tried to lose their attackers. Naik (Corporal) Premsingh Gurung, having killed a

Japanese soldier with his kukri, had been shot in the leg, shattering the bone. The men could not carry him and the area was infested with Japanese. This was precisely the type of situation Wingate had foreseen and the men had to face, that there was no option but to leave him. The young Gurkha was alone, wounded and not prepared to be captured. The Chindits marched on and a single shot rang out.

No. 1 Column advanced more prudently and reached the railway without being detected. They mined the lines and blew a railway bridge and moved to cross the Irrawaddy. At the same time, on 6 March, Calvert celebrated his 30th birthday with his Commandos by blowing up a couple of railway bridges spanning a *chaung* at Nankan, about 15 miles south-east of Pinlebu, and cut the railway in more than seventy places in the Nankan area. Calvert also directed his men to set up an ambush on the road running south between Nankan and Wuntho. Vehicles containing Japanese troops drove straight into the ambush and were hit by machine guns and mortars. In the fire-fight that followed, Calvert's men destroyed the enemy force, the so-called 'supermen of the jungle' without a single Chindit loss.

At the same time, Fergusson and 5 Column were also causing mayhem further east, near the Irrawaddy, at Bonchaung, where they were preparing to blow the railway bridge. Platoons from his column were engaged in various battles in the area, but he dispatched his main force to head to the railway. In one of the battles, John Kerr, the Welsh hand-to-hand fighting instructor, later to be imprisoned with Frank, was injured with a bullet in his calf. He was found near to several dead Japanese soldiers and a couple of dead British soldiers. Kerr and his men had surprised a truck of Japanese infantry in a village and opened fire, killing some of the enemy. As the truck sped off, Kerr and some of his men were hit with a light machine gun that had opened fire from another position.

Kerr and his comrades had killed sixteen Japanese, with one of the Gurkhas, Naik Jhuriman Rai having accounted for five of them, two with his kukri. Fergusson, however, was now faced with a problem he had dreaded: what to do with the wounded? Those who could be moved, including Kerr, were strapped to mules and taken to a nearby village. Two others, Sergeant Drummond and Corporal Johnson, were too bad to be moved and had to be left, with Kerr being told where they were. Both of them died from their wounds. From a diary that Kerr later wrote in Rangoon Jail, of the two men with him, Corporal Dale was murdered by Burmese. The villagers betrayed them to the Japanese and he and Private Bell were captured. Kerr, his wounds infested with worms, was violently interrogated for information. Bell died en route to Rangoon prison from the wound to his thigh and from the neglect of his captors.

Chapter Six

On the road to Mandalay
Where the flyin' fishes play
And the dawn comes up like thunder
Out of China 'cross the bay.

The Road to Mandalay,
Rudyard Kipling

I landed in Mandalay in October 2017. It was my starting-point to head north to Katha and then to cross the Irrawaddy to Inywa. The dawn in Mandalay was a dusty red and as I walked the streets, women had already laid out their mats covered with their produce and were starting to trade, and young monks in their maroon robes collected alms of rice, vegetables and meat in large, black clay pots, just as they have for generations.

From Mandalay I travelled eight hours north to Katha, passing roadside villages and farms, the houses and transport so similar to what Frank would have seen. Huts of bamboo on stilts, acres of forests and carts pulled by buffalo. We passed a procession of carved Buddha statues holding alms bowls built by the village. Small pagodas were built in fields, each with a Buddha inside, some in the position of prayer, some teaching, some cast in recline.

I knew of Katha from George Orwell's novel *Burmese Days*. Set around the British Club where, in his days as a policeman of the British Empire, Orwell wrote a bleak story in which there were no winners; where the rotting of the last days of British Rule is played out through the decay of the central characters. In the 1944 Operation THURSDAY, Chindits had been parachuted into Katha and fought in the surrounding areas.

Close to Katha, Wingate was deciding whether or not to cross the Irrawaddy. He had not heard news of 1 Group. No. 4 Column had returned to India and he was not sure of the conditions of 3 and 5 Columns. Then news began to come in. The main part of 1 Group had crossed the Irrawaddy and a report was brought in of the success of 3 Column. Fergusson made contact to say he considered that the conditions to cross were good and once on the other side of the Irrawaddy, he could march to the Shweli River suspension bridge and destroy it, cutting off Myitkyina, a town with a large Japanese occupation force and a strategically important airstrip. Calvert and 3 Column (who had now acquired an elephant and a *mahout* rider) were also keen to cross and radioed Wingate for permission to take 3 Column eastwards over the river.

Wingate, encouraged by the views of his commanders and considering there was still work that could be done, gave his consent. At the time, Japanese troops were being rapidly deployed into the area to respond to the demolitions and attacks on their patrols. No. 5 Column crossed at the village of Tigyaing, making it off the bank just in time to be out of range of the force of 200 Japanese who had arrived from the south moments later.

Calvert's column also hit trouble as they crossed. He had left a strong rearguard in place to protect the crossing and it was needed. Japanese soldiers, with strength in numbers, closed in on the crossing and engaged the rearguard and battle was joined. The rearguard managed to hold the far larger Japanese force at bay and kept them off the river bank, though only just. The engagement hurt the column: seven men were killed and six men – five Gurkhas and a Burma rifleman – were wounded and needed to be left at a Burmese village.

The brigade column, flanked by 7 and 8 Columns, had been using much of its time on propaganda, never missing an opportunity to enter villages, spend money and speak about positive British intentions for Burma and the threat of the Japanese. As Wingate spoke to villagers, aided by the interpreters of the Burma Rifles, Frank was deployed with the other Chindits to defensive positions, with Bren-gunners covering tracks into the villages, sharp eyes scanning the huts and tree lines for any cause for concern. Beyond testing his theory of long-distance penetration warfare, Wingate needed to gather intelligence. In the near future, a large British force would, he hoped, be sent to push the Japanese out of Burma. Knowing which villages could be trusted, knowing where wounded could be left or where sympathies would lie would prove to be critical for those who would follow the trail blazed by the men of Operation LONGCLOTH.

Brigade, 7 and 8 Columns now approached the Irrawaddy. At this stage, the number of animals accompanying the columns had been reduced. The *mahouts*, no doubt feeling that being fired upon was not in their job description, had already fled with their elephants. The horses simply could not cope. They were not made for the jungle, were malnourished and were suffering from exhaustion and injuries. It seems they had no hope of survival and the painful decision was taken to put the surviving horses down.

Wingate had received reports that the Japanese were sending troops from Katha and the paths would be patrolled. He avoided the patrols by taking his column over the mountains rather than around. After a gruelling march at full pace, they arrived at Hlwebo on the opposite bank of the town of Inywa. Wingate considered his options and resolved to cross. He wanted to gain experience of crossing wide and swift rivers and to gain valuable knowledge of the mostly uncharted land between the Irrawaddy and Shweli rivers.

Frank, like most, had complete confidence in Wingate, but there was certainly some grumbling in the ranks and some of the officers had private concerns. They were filthy and starting to feel the effects of short rations and the days of long marching over unforgiving territory. Still, they had been successful in their objectives so far and the men of the brigade were still confident and capable of operating. Some of the more astute and experienced soldiers had a sense of foreboding; there was a scarcity of information about the area, particularly concerning water sources. Further, they were going into the centre of a triangle, the sides of which were daunting obstacles: the Irrawaddy River, the Shweli River and the Japanese closing in, now fully aware of a comparatively small marauding force operating behind their lines.

* * *

To reach Inywa from Katha, I was told that there was no road down which a car could travel and so I would need to travel by motorbike on a dirt road. I was taken to a small roadside garage that rented out bikes. The bikes were all old and had been subjected to numerous repairs and I could not help but wonder if they would get me to the destination and back. I was offered a scooter, but I rejected it out of hand; not because it looked like it was falling apart or that the exhaust was fastened to the body of the machine with gaffer tape: the problem was that the seat was covered with the name and faded logo of Liverpool Football Club. As a lifelong Manchester United fan, I simply could not countenance it and said as much. Nobody seemed to understand my basis for refusing, but I was resolute and so I was given a small 125cc bike that had no allegiance to any club. It needed fuel, so a young lady working at the garage returned with a plastic bottle filled with fuel and, using a kitchen funnel, poured it into the tank and off I set, heading south.

The journey took about an hour. To the west, I was flanked by a high range of hills, covered in dense jungle over which Frank had trudged on his way to the Irrawaddy.

As I bumped and bounced along the road, the huts I passed were built from bamboo and latticed strips of wood, looking no different to the huts Frank would have passed seventy-four years earlier. Nor would the scenes I passed: a woman in an Asian rice hat, a bamboo pole across her shoulder with bundles of grasses tied to it, an old man leading a flock, or the woman holding a baby in the doorway of her hut.

I stopped en route at a roadside stall. The proprietor, in a white vest and with a broad smile, served me sweet tea. He worked with his two sons and wife. I asked if he had always lived there. He pointed to the hills ahead of me and to the west. 'Bonchaung,' he answered. 'Oh,' I replied, 'my grandfather's comrades blew up the bridge there; I hope

74

it hasn't caused too much inconvenience.' He seemed to find this very amusing and laughed loudly, although becoming more serious he went on to say that his parents had lived through the occupation and told him stories of the cruelties that had been endured by the local population. Men had been used as forced labour, there had been rapes of women and Japanese soldiers would routinely make civilians stand in front of them and repeatedly slapped their faces as an intended humiliation.

This was not the only time I heard of cruelty to civilians at the hands of the Japanese. Travelling through Shwebo, west of the Irrawaddy and to the north of Mandalay, I stopped for a leg-stretching break close to a farm. The family waved me to come over and invited me to sit on their veranda. Two young ladies seated beneath the grass-thatched roof of a separate open-sided, covered area were shelling peanuts from their harvest and filling large woven baskets. They came over with a large plate of nuts for me and I was joined by the father, his wife and several grandchildren. There were also two ladies, sisters in their 80s, who sat together at a wooden table in the shade. Both wore *lunghis* and traditional button-down collarless shirts and both had their hair tied up in severe buns. They had the lined faces of women who had led working lives in the sun. I was brought tea and jaggery, a sickly-sweet lump made of sugar cane and dates, and only then did this generous, genial family ask who I was and where I was travelling.

I told them about my grandfather and the purpose of my journey. One of the old ladies said she remembered when the Japanese came to occupy the village. As a child she found this exciting and wanted to see, but her father pulled her back and shouted at her to stay well away. The Japanese were not always there, but when they came through people were scared and she remembered men being taken away and demands for food. Her sister told me that she also remembered other soldiers coming through, with faces like she had not seen before, like mine. She was told they were British and recalled thinking they were very tall, but they did not stay and simply passed through.

Reaching the west bank of the river, there was a small collection of wooden huts with grass roofs. If the village has a name, it is not on the maps and nobody was able to tell me. It may be that this was Hlwebo from where the Chindits crossed over, but nobody in the village to whom I spoke could confirm this; it was simply where they lived and they didn't seem to need a name for it. Several villagers with bags, boxes and motorcycles were congregated near the bank waiting for the wooden sampan boat to return and ferry me over to Inywa. Some women were bathing in the Irrawaddy, their robes wrapped around them to preserve their modesty, while a couple of others sat on their haunches at the edge of the water with plastic bowls and piles of clothing to wash. Walking among the commuters and villagers were buffalo. As always, I was met with smiles and greetings of 'Mingele bar' as I walked around taking photographs. Further along on a jetty was a group of young children. The youngest girl was dressed as if going to church in her Sunday best, in a yellow frock with a frilly pink hat. They were throwing stones at a buffalo in the water, who didn't seem in the least concerned that it was being used for target practice.

Of the crossing itself, all Frank says is 'then we crossed the Irrawaddy'. The crossing, on 18 March, would have been a major undertaking, with approximately 1,200 men, radios, weapons and packs, and the mules. They piled into local boats and were paddled over by the skilled boatmen, with the crossing taking just over an hour.

The wooden sampan boat was fitted with an old outboard motor. It was a warm day. The water looked still, but that was just the surface. The current was strong. The river stretched far into the horizon with mountains rising in the distance. The brown-looking waters at the banks had now taken on a deeper blue as they reflected the sky. Never far from my mind was Frank. Was he over in one of the first boats to secure the beachhead with the other Bren-gunners and mortar teams, or was he one of the last as a rearguard was needed?

The boatman leaned over and tapped my arm. Pointing to a part in the river where the waters seemed to swell as two currents pressed together, he indicated to the west and said 'Irrawaddy', and then to the east of the swell 'Shweli' and then to where the waters were meeting. 'Irrawaddy, Shweli,' he said, bringing his hands together; the confluence of the two great rivers.

Intelligence had been received by Wingate that members of Aung San's Burmese Defence Army were stationed in the town of Inywa. The pro-Japanese militia were not trained and were poorly armed – capable of scaring unarmed farmers – but certainly they were not going to try to take on a heavily-armed and battle-hardened military force. Where they could do damage was by passing on intelligence to the Japanese. The Chindits quickly deployed to block the roads out of the village until the full force was across.

This is a village where visitors are limited to family and trade. Burma is a country with little tourism, even in 2017, and certainly compared to its neighbours, the tourist sites tend to be limited to the main cities and UNESCO Heritage sites such as the ancient city of Bagan with its thousands of pagodas spread through the landscape. Inywa is truly off the beaten track and news that a white Westerner had come to visit seemed to cause some interest.

I was met by four villagers who took me to meet U Myo Myint, a retired headmaster of the school and now a respected village elder, at his home a short distance away. The home was made of teak, with a picket fence and a corrugated metal roof. The front of the house was fully open with a small porch area leading directly into the main room, the floor of which was covered by large vinyl mats.

U Myo Myint sat cross-legged on the porch. He struck me at once as a decent man. Smartly dressed in a crisp, white collarless shirt and a checked black *lunghi*, his grey hair was neatly combed into a side parting and his expression was of intelligence and interest, tempered by patience. He was accompanied by a young teacher from the local school. He listened intently, without interruption, as I explained why I was there. As I spoke, a small group of villagers gathered round. I was told that I was the first Westerner to visit Inywa, certainly as long as anybody there could remember, and perhaps even since my grandfather had passed through. I asked U Myo Myint if he knew of anyone in the town who might be old enough to remember the Japanese occupation and perhaps the British passing through. He shook his head and told me that there was nobody. The village headman, who would certainly have recalled, had died just a couple of months before my visit. I felt a little irritated with myself that I had left it until now to make the trip rather than a year earlier. To the side of us, there was some discussion between the young teacher and a villager. The villager had told the teacher that there was a man living at the edge of the town who was a boy during the war and might remember. Without my asking, it was agreed that I would be taken there.

Accompanied by the teacher, U Myo Myint and seven or eight of the villagers on scooters and motorcycles, we set off together through the village, riding down the dusty earth roads past the wooden and bamboo huts with roofs of grasses and fenced gardens filled with vegetable plots and fruit trees, past scenes and sights so similar to those seen by Frank.

A teenage girl came out to greet me as I approached the dusty street I had been directed to. I explained that my grandfather had passed through here when he was a soldier and that I was looking to speak to an old man who had lived then. She was very pleased to welcome me. This was her family home and the man I wanted to speak to was her grandfather, U Tun Sein. She ushered me around the corner to the other side of her house where he was sitting in the open-fronted room. The house, with walls made of thin strips of wood criss-crossed into a lattice, was built on stilts, so as I stood, the old man sitting before me on the floor was at the same height as me. He didn't seem at all surprised to see me and just nodded his agreement slowly as his granddaughter introduced me and asked if he would speak with me.

U Tun Sein was unsure of his age; probably in his mid to late 80s, he thought, and would have been somewhere between 10 and 14 during the years that the Japanese were in occupation of Burma. He was then a novice monk. Most young Buddhist boys would spend at least a few weeks or months as a novice, to learn about their faith and how to behave towards monks and in temples. Some will spend longer and for some it will be their calling. U Tun Sein was living in a monastery that was garrisoned by the Japanese. He said the Japanese did not cause them any problems and were respectful to the monks. He remembered being very excited when his friend told him that British soldiers had come to the town. He didn't feel scared but was anxious to see them so walked from the monastery to get a closer look. He correctly remembered that they were not there for long.

Saying goodbye to U Tun Sein, he told me he had not seen a British man since that time as a young monk and now, he remarked, as I spoke with him and his granddaughter, it was fitting that it was the grandson of one of the soldiers who had come back.

I felt a deep sadness as the boat pushed along against the current on my return journey. This was the crossing Frank had not made. His desperate attempts to make it back across failed and his failure was punished by unimaginable horror.

* * *

After a bivouac at Inywa, Frank had moved out the following day to head southwards over the Shweli River and, with his column, they pressed on towards Baw, about 130 miles south from Inywa, passing through forested hills. The lack of water was now a major problem. The whole area was dry and water was hard to find. In the heat and under the weight of their packs, the men had to carefully conserve their water and began to suffer the effects of dehydration. They were exhausted from days of marching, constant stress of jungle warfare where the enemy could ambush at any moment and from their numerous skirmishes and battles. Furthermore, rations were running low and the men were not taking in anything like the daily calories they needed. All of this was affecting their fighting capabilities. The men were infested with lice and morale was falling. It was now abundantly clear that the situation was becoming very dangerous with Japanese troops having been brought into the area by road; they were now patrolling through the countryside and skirmishes were reported daily.

The Japanese now had a far clearer idea of the size, methods and capability of the British force and knew they were east of the Irrawaddy.

They began to move troops to occupy the villages on the river. Fatefully for Frank, one of these was Twinnge.

Wingate ordered a supply drop and wanted to use the opportunity to meet with the column commanders. The brigade column, flanked by Major Gilkes' 7 Column and Major Scott's 8 Column, having been through a number of battles, made it through the jungle to Baw on 23 and 24 March. The following day Jeffries' and Fergusson's columns heard the sounds of Wingate's force in heavy fighting with the Japanese and raced quickly to link up with the brigade column after cat-and-mouse games through the jungle with Japanese patrols.

Baw is a large area of fields and farms within surrounding hills and forests. The RAF had done all they could to throw the enemy off course by making fake supply drops, including dropping mail. The aim was to make the Japanese believe that the Chindits were planning an attack on Maymyo. The planned supply drop required the area to be closed off first, and then the village could easily be taken, held in dominating numbers and cleared of enemy. To do this the Chindits needed to close off the village by blocking all the routes in the surrounding areas. Patrols were sent out with orders to block the roads during the night, with all patrols to be in place by first light. Had this been achieved, the Japanese company occupying the village could have been taken by surprise.

No. 17 Platoon was under the command of Captain Coughlan and had been sent to block off tracks to the village. Encountering difficult jungle en route to their objective, the captain made a serious error and allowed his men to rest and sleep, believing that he would be able to use first light to better find their way through and still be in time to close off the tracks. Spotted by Japanese sentries, one of the Chindits opened fire. The sounds of gunfire brought men from the Japanese force that had been garrisoned nearby to support their sentries.

The Chindits split into three sections and took up defensive positions on the crest of a rise. The area was thick with jungle and visibility was no more than 10 yards. Seconds after the Chindits took their position, the Japanese opened up with their machine guns and battle was joined.

Orde Wingate, British Mandate Palestine, 1938.

Private Frank Berkovitch, India, 1942.

Private Frank Berkovitch (far left), with men of the 13th King's Regiment, India, 1942.

Jhansi Fort, where Wingate based his training HQ.

Abchand Jungle, India.

Gadheri River flowing through the Abchand Jungle.

Frank's son Tony in the Orchha Jungle: *'Jungle as it should be.'*

The Betwa River, where the Chindits trained in river crossing, at the edge of the Orchha Jungle with the palaces of Orchha in the background.

Orde Wingate, shortly after the conclusion of Operation LONGCLOTH, 1943.

No. R/CAS/169

(If replying, please quote above No.)

RECORD OFFICE
15 JUL 1943
PRESTON

Record Office,

_____19 .

SIR OR MADAM,

I regret to have to inform you that a report has been received from

the War Office to the effect that (No. 3780027 (Rank) Private

(Name) BERKOVITCH. F.

(Regiment) 13th Bn. The King's Regiment

was posted as " missing " on the date not yet known in the Indian

Theatre of War.

The report that he is missing does not necessarily mean that he has been killed, as he may be a prisoner of war or temporarily separated from his regiment.

Official reports that men are prisoners of war take some time to reach this country, and if he has been captured by the enemy it is probable that unofficial news will reach you first. In that case I am to ask you to forward any postcard or letter received at once to this Office, and it will be returned to you as soon as possible.

Should any further official information be received it will be at once communicated to you.

I am,

SIR OR MADAM,

Mrs Sarah Berkovitch,   Your obedient Servant,
    32, Greenstead Avenue,
        Crumpsall,
            Manchester 10.

                          Major.
                Officer in charge of Records.

IMPORTANT.

Any change of your address should be immediately notified to this Office.

Wt. 30051/1249   400,000   (16)   9/39   KJL/8812   Gp 698/3   Forms/B.104—83/9

Letter from the Records Office to Sarah Berkovitch, 15 July 1943, informing her that Frank was reported as 'missing' in the Indian theatre of war.

Letter from Major General Wingate to Sarah Berkovitch, 10 November 1943.

The railway in Pyin Oo Lwin (formerly Maymyo) with the servants' quarters in the background. This is close to where the captured Chindits were held.

Old servants' quarters building in Pyin Oo Lwin (formerly Maymyo). The PoWs were likely to have been held in huts in these grounds.

A hut in the village of Waw, close to where Frank and the Pegu marchers were liberated.

U Chow in Waw village. As a boy he lived through the Japanese occupation and recalled British soldiers fighting against the Japanese at the end of the war, assisted by men from the village.

Recently liberated prisoner of war at Rangoon Jail, May 1945.

Mug shots of medical orderlies from Rangoon Jail, with Lieutenant Akio Onishi in the prominent photo, from the War Crimes file. Onishi denied medication and equipment to prisoners and caused deaths through cruelty and negligence.

Columns of names of 26,855 soldiers with no known graves at the Taukkyan Commonwealth War Cemetery.

Taukkyan Commonwealth War Cemetery which contains 6,374 graves from the Second World War, 867 of which are unknown. The columns are engraved with the names of 26,855 service personnel who have no known graves.

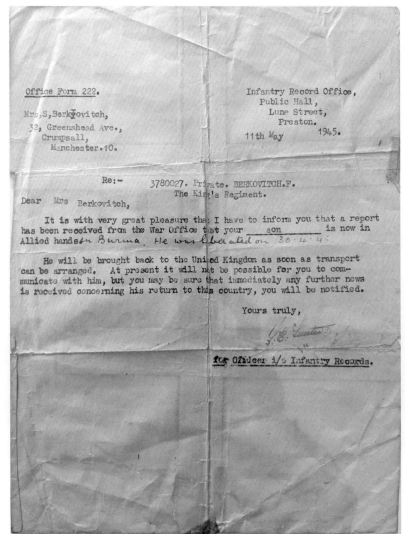

Office Form 222.

Mrs.S.Berkovitch,
32, Greenshead Ave.,
Crumpsall,
Manchester.10.

Infantry Record Office,
Public Hall,
Lune Street,
Preston.
11th May   1945.

Re:-   3780027. Private. BERKOVITCH.F.
               The King's Regiment.

Dear Mrs Berkovitch,

It is with very great pleasure that I have to inform you that a report has been received from the War Office that your ____ son ____ is now in Allied hands *in Burma. He was liberated on 30·4·45*

He will be brought back to the United Kingdom as soon as transport can be arranged.   At present it will not be possible for you to communicate with him, but you may be sure that immediately any further news is received concerning his return to this country, you will be notified.

Yours truly,

for Officer i/c Infantry Records.

Letter from the Infantry Record Office to Sarah Berkovitch, 11 May 1945, informing her that Frank had been liberated and was in Allied hands.

The Chindit force was heavily outnumbered and suffered immediate casualties, with one private killed and several injured in the firing.

The main force was 4 miles away preparing the drop zone. They heard the fire and men from 7 and 8 Columns were dispatched as reinforcements and to take the village.

The fighting was desperate and close. The Chindits were holding off the Japanese with hand grenades, but they could not hold them for long. The Japanese had fire and numerical supremacy and were using mortars and machine guns to keep the Chindits, now short on ammunition, pinned down, as their infantry crawled below the fire ready to charge the British platoons with their bayonets. The British had no ammunition to waste and had to fire only when a target presented itself. One Japanese soldier was shot by an officer as he bore down on a wounded Bren-gunner with his bayonet. He came so close that if he had fallen forward in death instead of backwards, he would have skewered the Chindit.[1]

No. 15 Platoon, led by the famed Captain Petersen, 'The Fighting Dane', came to the rescue, having raced to the battle. Ultimately, the Chindits prevailed in the fight and the Japanese suffered heavy casualties, with their company either killed, wounded or forced to retreat from the area. Captain Petersen was wounded by a bullet to his head, but his men were not prepared to abandon him. He was strapped to a horse and made a full recovery and eventually marched out of Burma.

The original plan was to use dried paddy fields as the drop zone, but this had to be changed at the last minute. Wingate decided he needed to capture the village at this stage and sent in fighting platoons from the columns at Baw to do the job. It may be that Frank was in this attack; if not, he would have been holding a defensive position or among the men cutting a clearing and hastily lighting a flare path in the jungle for the new drop zone.

If Frank was among the men who entered the village he, like the others, would have noticed that it was quiet, too quiet; suddenly accurate fire broke out from inside a hut, killing two men. The Chindits raked the hut with Brens and hit it with mortars, killing all the occupants. Using hand grenades and Sten guns, the enemy was cleared from the huts in the villages. The main Japanese force had retreated to the east into the jungle, but men from 7 and 8 Columns caught them. At the conclusion of the battle, the Chindits had lost the two men killed in the village to more than 200 Japanese killed.[2] The area was now safe for the RAF to make their drop.

Baw is one of the places in Burma that I was unable to visit. I had hoped to travel there from Katha, but was told that there were only two routes there: one required special permission to travel through, and the other was impassable as the road had been badly damaged in the monsoon rains a few months earlier and had not been repaired. My guide and interpreter Ko Soe Win had made enquiries and called a contact who lived in the nearby area. The Burmese are deeply superstitious, with a firm belief, certainly among devotees of the Buddha, in reincarnation and in the overlapping of the spirit dimensions with the human dimension. There was a trace of concern in Ko Soe Win's voice as he told me: 'Baw is gone…. Everybody fled – there were sounds at night, people screaming, sounds of people working…. It is a village of ghosts.'

The drop was light. Two days' rations for each man, including bully beef, beans and rum, but at least it was something. Throughout the campaign, the men were very low on rations and had to supplement their diet with whatever they could buy in villages or kill in the jungle – python had become quite popular – and the bullocks that accompanied the columns were being slaughtered as needed. Foraging, though, was not easy. Unless in large numbers, such as at Baw, the columns were relying on speed and silence and rarely had time to stop and hunt. The physical exertion was huge and the men were malnourished and losing body weight quickly.

Wingate now needed to consider his next steps. He was aware that the mission was taking a huge toll on his men. The year was drawing towards its hottest period and the monsoon rains, which would make the rivers impassable, were approaching but he felt there were still important objectives to achieve. He wanted Calvert to blow the bridge over the Gokteik Gorge and Wingate wanted to take his column into the Kachin Hills to link up with Captain 'Fish' Herring, his intelligence officer who had been stirring up support for a rebellion among the Kachins.

Wingate's decision was ultimately made for him in India. The RAF simply could not fly far enough to make more distant supply drops and were already operating at their limits. This, combined with other factors and the importance of getting intelligence back to India for future missions led to him being given the order to withdraw and get out of Burma.

Chapter Seven

'O, I have suffer'd
With those that I saw suffer: a brave vessel,
Who had, no doubt, some noble creature in her,
Dash'd all to pieces. O, the cry did knock
Against my very heart! Poor souls, they perished.'

The Tempest, William Shakespeare

For all the Chindits, the journey would take them to the limits of human endurance. In attempting to escape from Burma some of the Chindits would make it out, some would be captured, and some would be left behind and never heard of again. Some would die from bullets, some from exhaustion, from drowning, or from wounds. Some would die under torture or of disease or neglect or murder after capture. Some would survive captivity. Every single man would suffer adversity, deprivation and misery, which cannot be fathomed by anyone who did not share in these hardships.

When they entered Burma, the Chindits were among the fittest men in the British army, but it was not just their fitness that saw them take their places in Operation LONGCLOTH, it was also their resilience and willingness to endure hardship, their grit and mental stamina. At this stage, as they prepared to leave, their bodies were wasting from malnutrition, they were filthy and riddled with lice, their muscles exhausted from marching many hundreds of miles through harsh terrain and their nerves tested from the constant risks they faced. They had done all that was required of them so far, destroying the railway line in multiple places, harassing and killing numerous enemy, drawing large Japanese forces away from other front lines and collecting information which would be of enormous value to any future expeditions into Burma. They were no longer capable of fighting and marching as they had been. Exhausted to the point that all they had now was their determination, resourcefulness and the will to get back, their final job was to get the intelligence they had gathered back to British lines. They would now need to avoid confrontations with Japanese troops. Survival would depend on speed, cunning and silence.

The news that they were to get out of Burma didn't cause any outbreak of joy. It was more a sense of relief, attenuated by a feeling that it would not be so easy to turn their backs on the jungle that had become integral to their lives. Frank gives no sense in his memoir of how he felt. He would have had some apprehension, aware that between him and India were two wide, raging rivers, often impassable jungle, a very angry enemy, poor water supplies and many, many miles. Supply drops could not be counted on as the forces could now not so easily secure an area, speed was so important and villages would need to be avoided as much as possible to reduce the risk of betrayal. The journey out was going to be fraught with every conceivable danger the jungle and the enemy could throw at them.

Wingate had advised the column commanders that when the time came to disperse, the dispersal groups should number about forty men each. At first though, 7, 8 and Brigade would move together towards Inywa. Wingate believed that the last thing the Japanese would expect would be for them to cross back at the same point as when they had moved to the east. In this, however, he was wrong.

The columns set off towards Inywa, with Wingate leading and adeptly navigating the route: a march of 50 miles that needed to be covered quickly before the Japanese could work out their intentions. Another danger was also approaching: the monsoon rains were imminent, which would make the rivers even more lethal. Wingate ordered that most heavy equipment be destroyed and dumped, and all but the healthiest mules be killed. Where possible, the mules would be used for meat, but in most cases it was simply because the poor animals were too exhausted and were slowing the columns down. The painful job fell to the animal transport officers. The ATOs were ordered to lead the mules off from the rest of the column. The morale of the men was under severe strain and they had all grown fond of the mules. They were to be killed out of sight. However, for the men tasked to kill them, it could not be done quickly with a bullet. Wingate was concerned about the noise and ordered that they be killed silently. This was done with a bayonet. The youngest of the ATOs, Bill Smyly, would return to the men with tears streaming down his face. After he had killed the mules which stood no chance of survival in the unforgiving jungle, he reached his limit and turned the rest free.

The force arrived at Inywa, not knowing whether there were Japanese soldiers on the opposite bank and in what strength. Furthermore, there was a danger that the Chindits could be attacked from the rear if they had been tracked. The Burma Rifles were to collect boats, following which 7 Column would cross to form a bridgehead on the western side to hold the area so that the others could cross.

Major Fergusson's column, two days' march behind, would provide protection for the crossing as the rearguard; in his own words, 'the place of honour.'[1] It may have been the place of honour, but with that came danger. Nerves were taut and there was an awareness that the Japanese were closing in. Fergusson directed his officers that in the event of his death, they should seek an audience on his behalf with Wavell and underline his firm view that this type of warfare was feasible and effective.

Fergusson decided to move off to the east and lead any pursuing Japanese away from Inywa. He took 5 Column down a dry riverbed, making noise and leaving an obvious false trail. They made a false bivouac, setting large fires to attract the Japanese. Any Imperial soldiers who entered the bivouac would stand a good chance of setting off one of the booby-traps the Chindits laid as welcoming gifts.

After carefully covering their tracks out, they bivouacked half a mile away (with no fires) about a mile from Hintha, a jungle village about 20 miles south-east of Inywa. The plan had been to surround the village, but the jungle around it was impassable with thick bamboo and thorns.

The only way in was along the main track. The men approached with hand grenades in their hands.

Fergusson scouted ahead with two Burrifs. He spotted a group of men sitting around a fire. 'Burmese', thought Fergusson as he approached. As he got closer, he realized they were Japanese and tossed a grenade into the fire. Philip Stibbe heard him shout 'Take that and share it among you', followed by an explosion as the grenade detonated and shattered shrapnel tore into the bodies of the enemy.[2] Seconds later machine-gun fire erupted and Stibbe gave the order to fix bayonets and split his men into three sections to the left and right of him and with himself leading the central section. Machine guns opened up on the Chindits. Stibbe threw a grenade at the nearest gun and hit the ground. As he got up, he was shot in the chest, just below the collarbone. Fergusson was hit by grenade shrapnel as he came to speak to the wounded Stibbe and several other men were wounded in the fighting. At least six Chindits were killed; a heavy loss, although the Japanese had taken far higher casualties. Stibbe ordered his men to leave him behind. A Burmese Rifleman, Maung Tun, volunteered to stay with the officer. Hidden together in the jungle, Stibbe's wound was treated by the Burrif. Maung Tun left to meet a villager who had agreed to provide them with food and information about whether the Japanese had moved on from the village. Tun was betrayed, tortured and, when he refused to reveal the location of the wounded officer, shot. Eventually, desperate for water, Stibbe gathered the strength to move and retraced his steps back to Hintha, armed with just a hand grenade. As he staggered into the village, he found it was still occupied by the Japanese and he was quickly captured. He would face two years of imprisonment, suffering in the same jails, at the hands of the same guards and walking the same road to freedom as Frank.

As Fergusson's men were paying the price in blood to protect the main force at Hintha, Frank was awaiting his turn to cross the Irrawaddy. The first two platoons from 7 Column began to cross. There were only six rowing boats to take the men across so the crossing would not be quick as the boats would need to return repeatedly to collect the next group of anxious men. Chindit eyes scanned the far shore for the enemy as the first wave of boats set off. However, the Chindits were not the only ones watching and as the boats reached the far shore, Japanese troops, from the cover of the dense jungle, opened up with machine guns and mortars. One of the boats was hit with all its occupants killed.[3] Unable to turn back, the boats pressed on, with the Burmese boatmen paddling with all their strength. The Chindits on the east bank replied with everything they had. This was enough to protect the men in the boats as the enemy now pointed their fire at the east bank and away from the small vessels which were able to move downstream and reach the west bank. Sixty-five men made it across, crawling up the shore and dashing into the cover of the jungle.

The Japanese force had not been large: about sixty strong. However, Wingate had received reports that a few miles upstream was a large Japanese garrison who would by now be aware that a large British force had congregated at Inywa. He decided that now was the time to disperse. Frank simply wrote: 'We then got the orders to pull out in small parties so we would be sure that many of the men would reach India and get the information back where it mattered.'

Not everybody agreed with the brigadier's decision to disperse. There were about 700 men on the eastern shore. One platoon had already made it and they could have forced their way across in strength, though not without casualties. One lieutenant was scathing, saying he could never forgive Wingate for taking them so far but not for taking them all the way back.[4]

The columns were split into groups, each commanded by an officer or non-commissioned officer. The remaining heavy kit was discarded, including the Vickers guns and mortars which were first rendered inoperable. The men would be armed with rifles or Tommy guns and grenades, with Bren guns as their heaviest weapons. This was now a desperate race to make it out as each column, each dispersal party and each man weighed up the options and risks.

The commanders of each column and each dispersal group began to plan their escape. Some would try to head for the British-held outpost of Fort Hertz, situated north towards China, and then along the border towards the entrance to the Himalayas. Others would aim for China and the majority opted to travel back towards the Chindwin. The pre-monsoon land was dry and water hard to come by. The groups were either finding a place to cross the Irrawaddy or Shweli. Some made it across without interference and headed on to the Chindwin or to the north. The rations were now gone. The only food was jungle roots, buffalo or mule meat and anything they caught – usually python – or managed to buy in villages, invariably rice. Some men kept themselves moving with amphetamine tablets which came with a supply drop.[5]

The first man out from the expedition was Flight Lieutenant Robert Thompson who crossed over with his group on 14 April and they were picked up by a patrol of the British army. Thompson was awarded the Military Cross.

Calvert followed soon after. He arranged an air drop of machine guns and rations and split off towards India. Weary and fighting engagements on their way back, they made it across the Chindwin to the British lines. In their wake, 3 Column left a staggering enemy body count and destroyed more infrastructure than any other column. Calvert brought out more of his men alive than any other column commander, together with vital intelligence, but not all his men made it back to British lines. A lieutenant in 3 Column, commanding a group of Gurkha Rifles, was Denis Gudgeon. After getting his men across the Irrawaddy, they struck out for the Chindwin. He had no map and relied on a compass bearing. After miles of marching, the malnourished officer could not go on. He ordered the young Gurkhas under his command to leave him behind rather than risk their lives by slowing them down. Recovering some strength, he went on alone. He found a Burmese boatman near to the Chindwin. The boatman promised to take him over, but took him first to a village. Gudgeon was put in a hut and told to wait. He was betrayed by the Burmese boatman and would spend two years in Rangoon Jail. Many years later a recording was made of his memories. One of those memories is of Frank. It was a memory that left me with my head in my hands.

Fergusson's 5 Column suffered devastating losses. Of the 318 men who went in, fewer than one in three made it out, almost a quarter were killed and 86 became PoWs, of whom just 27 survived. The crossing of the Shweli with his column was hellish; some men lost their footing and were swept away into the darkness of the night and drowned. A large group of men lost their nerve on a sandbank and could not bring themselves to get back into the water. The light of dawn was not much more than an hour away and Fergusson was sure Japanese patrols would be in the area. He had a decision to make: stay and attempt to find ways to get the remaining men across or leave them. If he stayed, it was likely that the entire column would shortly be outnumbered and find itself in a battle with the Japanese patrols. He calculated that if he moved, the men who had risked their lives and crossed over from the sandbank could be saved. The ones who remained could not. It came down to simple mathematics. More would live if he moved on. It was a decision he knew to be the right one, but it haunted him all of his days.[6]

In one of the smaller dispersal groups was the other Jewish tailor, Leon Frank. Heading to Fort Hertz, his group escaped a Japanese patrol and their lieutenant decided the group was too large, so he and five others broke off and decided to head east for China, living like bandits, holding up villagers at gunpoint and demanding food. Finding a hut on a hillside, they went in to rest, all too exhausted to have even thought of posting a guard. A Japanese soldier rushed through and stabbed one of the men through the hand. They were ordered out by a Japanese officer and found themselves surrounded by Imperial soldiers. A machine gun was pointed at them and the men believed they were about to be shot in cold blood, but these Japanese soldiers were of the disciplined and well-trained Imperial Guard. They secured and bound the small group of Chindits and they were led off into captivity.

For those who went north, journeying into the hills, they dodged and sometimes engaged Japanese patrols. Kachin tribesmen guided them to friendly villages, feeding them, resting them and then moving them on, away from Japanese patrols until they were safely in the hands of Chinese allies.

A group under a highly-respected officer, Major Scott, had radioed for a supply drop. When they arrived at the drop zone, it was found to be a flat run of land in a 'T'-shape in a clearing of jungle. It was 1,200 yards long and 300 yards wide. By now, Scott had a large number of wounded with him and doubted he could get them out. They found a large area and used what materials they could to spell out 'Plane land here now, wounded'. The pilots making the supply drop saw the message and dropped a note telling them to hold on.

Two days later, escorted by fighter planes, an RAF pilot – apparently with ice running through his veins – made the hazardous landing on his second pass. Nineteen men were to be loaded on board. As one of the men, Sergeant Burt Fitton, prepared to board, he turned to his commander: 'I'm alright Sir. I came in on my feet, and I'd like to go out the same way.'[7] He stepped aside and the remaining eighteen wounded men were loaded onto the Dakota. The plane rolled along the ground, picking up speed to take off as the trees loomed ahead. The pilot pulled up; it was close. The weight of a nineteenth man could have been too much. They cleared the treetops by just inches and two hours later the wounded, whose death was almost certain had they not been airlifted, were in a hospital in Imphal. Sergeant Fitton marched on. A few days later he was dead, killed in an ambush.

For the men remaining in the jungle, the monsoon rains were now starting to arrive in fits and starts, but when it rained, it was a deluge. Dispersal groups avoided Japanese patrols where they could, or ambushed where it was the best option. One group ambushed a convoy of four trucks with the Bren guns giving the leading truck the bad news. The vehicle left the road, overturned and then burst into flames. The remaining three trucks and their occupants were also destroyed. The missing section could not be found and it was presumed they had been taken prisoner. Although they suffered casualties, they inflicted a far higher toll on the enemy. At other times the Chindits, their instincts dulled by hunger, dehydration and fatigue, were ambushed and pursued through the jungle. Starving, some men found and killed a buffalo, eating the flesh raw rather than waiting for a fire to be lit.

Wingate split the brigade column into five dispersal groups, one of which he commanded himself. To which group Frank was assigned and whether he was with Wingate is unclear, lost in the fog of time. The dispersal groups from Brigade prepared to leave. They worked rapidly; killing and skinning some of the remaining mules, they quickly cooked the meat. Frank filled his water bottles, ate what he could and packed some of the meat for the journey ahead.

The men stripped their kit to a minimum. Weapons, ammunition, food and water were the essentials. After that the men had to work out what could be discarded and how much weight their malnourished bodies could manage to carry. The escape maps were crude as so much of the Burmese interior was uncharted; they were all they had. Frank and his dispersal group discussed routes and prepared to set out on whichever path they thought would give the best way out. All were aware that on all sides the Japanese were closing in, they were heavily outnumbered, ammunition was low, they had minimal supplies, the monsoon rains were coming and there were major natural obstacles to negotiate over hundreds of miles.

Wingate's dispersal group decided to move off into a bivouac to take stock, plan a route and rest for a while before they moved south to look, over several days, for another crossing. He reached Maunggon and secured three boats. As they were crossing, Wingate's group came under fire. The native boatmen fled, leaving half the party on the eastern bank. Wingate's party then consisted of him, four other officers and twenty-four other ranks; a total of twenty-nine men. It is possible that Frank was one of those left behind.

Wingate took the remainder of his group and, avoiding tracks wherever they could, hacked a path through the jungle. After marching for two days, they came to the railway which was now being heavily patrolled. Conscious of the noise of breaking bamboo and teak branches, the Chindits moved slowly to the edge of the jungle. The railway at this point cut through the jungle, so the forest continued 10 yards on from the railway line on the other side. Wingate dispatched scouts who reported seeing enemy pickets a few hundred yards away in both directions. They decided to make a run for it. Bunched together, Wingate led his troops over the line and into the jungle undetected. Pressing forward, they slipped again through the Japanese forces around Pinbon and Pinlebu, where Japanese garrisons had been attacked on the way in. Their rations were now depleted and they ate what they could scavenge from the jungle.

Wingate made it to the Chindwin, but the Japanese had been patrolling the east bank and removed boats. Wingate formed a plan. With his strongest swimmers he would swim the Chindwin at a place where there had been reports of British troops, and then return with boats for the others. With the rest of the dispersal group hidden in the jungle, Wingate, with Aung Thin, his tough Burmese captain, Sergeant Wilshaw, Private Boardman, Major Jeffries and Sergeant John Carey set off, hidden by elephant grass. As they were travelling in daylight and had to move imperceptibly, and as the grass was stiff with knife-sharp edges and well above the height of a man, their progress was slow, taking several hours to cover just a few hundred yards.

They stripped, tied their boots to their packs and, expecting the possibility of a fight on the other side, carried their rifles overhead as they waded into the river. The current was too strong to fight and the best they could do was to kick out in the direction they wanted. Aung Thin got into difficulties and Boardman, seeing the Burrif going under, grabbed him and held on, kicking them both across. Wingate's indomitable strength was finally failing and he struggled to keep his head above water. His revolver belt was pulling him under and he managed to unfasten it and let it sink to the riverbed. Then feet touched the riverbed and they were through. Wading out of the water and racing into cover, they found a Burmese boatman who told Aung Thin that there was a British post 4 miles away.

A couple of hours later, five Chindits and their brigadier reached British lines. It was 28 April. The major in charge of the post organized a patrol to collect the remaining men on the eastern bank. Wingate insisted on joining the rescue party.

Other dispersal groups from Wingate's Brigade Column were less fortunate. Major Raymond Ramsay, the medical officer for the brigade column was captured in an ambush west of the Irrawaddy. Ramsay would be taken, like Frank, to the brutal Maymyo prison camp and they would be together in Rangoon. 'My word, he saved a lot of men...' Frank would say of him, and he did. He would suffer unimaginably in captivity, but would never give up. While it is hard to place someone's suffering on the scales, the fact is that but for Ramsay's capture, many more prisoners would have died. Only he can know if that was worth the misery he endured.

As for Frank, after leaving Inywa, his memoir becomes more detailed. The first part of his account mentions nothing really of the training and is scant on his part in the expedition before the Dispersal Order, but he is more forthcoming about his attempt to escape Burma and his imprisonment:

> My party moved south to the Irrawaddy and tried to cross. There was just one boat, which took half the men over while we waited for the boat to return. The current was too strong for two men to bring the boat back, so the rest of us marched on for about seven miles to another village, but found the Japs there. We moved back into the jungle and then moved on through with little hope of getting out of Burma.

Frank and the remainder of his group hastily planned what to do. They decided to continue south of Inywa, desperately looking for a place to cross. They melted into the relative safety of the jungle, but needed to break cover to inspect stretches of the unyielding river and look for boats. Their food was finished and the men were shattered. Water was low and becoming hard to find. Whereas in the early days of the journey when the men were fit and strong, a swipe of a *dah* would be enough to remove obstacles in the jungle, now they had to hack several times. Each swing ate into their reserves, each step took a cumulative toll, each sound was a potential enemy and a drain on their shredded nerves. Their morale was at rock bottom, but they kept going. The alternatives were unthinkable.

They approached a village, crawling forward and watching, weapons at the ready. 'Japs,' hissed one of the men, and Frank and the others froze. They crawled silently back into cover. On they went, further south, losing hope, beneath an ominous sky as monsoon clouds began to flex their muscles, walking on alongside the unforgiving Irrawaddy:

> With all our food gone and very little water left we were exhausted from moving through the thick jungle and found our progress was very slow. After a short rest we moved on again and came upon tracks of an elephant, which we followed to a pool of filthy water. We put some in our mess tins and boiled the water before we drank it.

I remember my grandfather telling this story when I was a child. He told me that he tracked elephants and 'drank a puddle of elephant pee'. Being a young boy, I thought this story was brilliant and, as I remember, he laughed about it.

Frank reached Twinnge, 60 miles as the crow flies from Inywa, but they would not have moved in a straight line. They would have cut through jungle, at best using game trails, avoiding paths and roads. Frank did not know the name. It was just another village. It would contain redemption or damnation. In their desperate condition they had to roll the dice and approach the village:

> We then moved on and came to another village, but we did not approach the village right away in case there were any Japanese there. After a while we started to move forward very slowly, our Sergeant was leading us in front, then from out of nowhere the Japs seemed to spring out from everywhere. Many of the men were wounded and the Sergeant got killed, with the rest of us captured.

Major Menzies-Anderson was an officer with the brigade column who made it out of Burma. He prepared a report document that contained the names of Brigade HQ soldiers who had not returned. Among the short list of names are two sergeants. One, James Masterton, would survive two years with Frank in Rangoon. The other sergeant on the list, Ed Burrows, is very likely to have been Frank's sergeant, shot to death in this ambush. I have searched records to try to find any family he may have to let them know what I now know, but could find no trace. All I could find was the record held at the Commonwealth War Graves Commission:

Service Number 3781648
Died Between 31/03/1943 and 24/04/1943
Aged 25
13th Bn.
The King's Regiment (Liverpool)
Son of Tom and Edith Burrows; husband of Eunice Burrows, of Swinton, Lancashire.

Ed Burrows has no known grave. Probably he was buried in an unmarked place in Twinnge. His name is high up on one of the columns which stand sentinel over more than 6,400 graves at the Rangoon Memorial located in the centre of Taukkyan War Cemetery. His name is engraved in stone, along with 26,855 other soldiers of the British Empire who died during the campaigns in Burma but have no known graves. Like Frank, he had come from Manchester. They trained together, marched together, fought side by side, found themselves stranded and abandoned on the wrong side of the Irrawaddy. They planned their escape together. In desperation they searched for food and water, they shared food and water, fears and hopes as they hid under the canopy of the undergrowth. Together they bivouacked through cold nights and together crept up to the tiny village in their anxious bid to secure food and a boat. Also, being a true sergeant, he led his men into this village from the front, knowing only too well that it may be occupied. His leadership and courage to go into that cursed village at the front of his men rather than sending someone else in first cost him his life. I stood below his name, engraved too high on the stone memorial to reach out and touch. Silently, I thanked him. I am not sure what I thanked him for, but I did. I don't know why because the words did not match my emotions. I just know that as I struggled to hold my composure at the foot of the memorial, overwhelmed by the rows and rows of graves, I looked up at his name, among so many, and said 'Thank you'.

In October 2017, I was turned back from Twinnge. I was tense as we approached. In the jungle that flanked the dusty road on which we travelled, Frank and the men of his dispersal group made their fateful gamble and crept out of the tree line. Somewhere near here bullets missed Frank, but wounded his comrades and killed his sergeant. Somewhere near here, he was led into captivity.

As the car in which I had travelled reached the entrance to the village, we were stopped at a checkpoint at the crest of a hill from where a road led down towards the village and the Irrawaddy.

A security official came to the car and leaned in through the open window. He stank of alcohol and did not seem particularly surprised to see me. I was told I needed special permission as the area is within a militarized zone. He was aggressive and demanded that my guide hand over my passport. I refused. Burma is not a country where I would find it easy to get a replacement as there is no British Embassy. 'Tell him no chance. He is drunk. He is not having it. Tell him to sod off.' Ko Soe Win followed the official into his small office by the barrier and may or may not have translated; certainly his voice was more placatory than mine and they spoke at some length. Either way, I held on to my passport, but we were told to turn around. As we did so, we could see the official gesticulating and shouting into a phone; we drove off quickly. It would not do for me to be arrested in the same place where my grandfather was taken prisoner.

* * *

The Chindits who made it over the Chindwin were all taken to a hospital in Imphal. Most had lost at least a quarter of their body weight and some far more. They were taken into the care of Matron McGeary, the recipient herself of a gallantry award for her heroism in treating the wounded at Dunkirk. She was adored by them. Like the Chindits, she had little respect for rules and would steal supplies for them: beer, chocolate, cigarettes, whatever they wanted. She would crack jokes with them, mother them and argue with any authority that got in her way. The matron was made a Member of the British Empire for her dedication to the Chindits in her care.

The men's clothes were burned, they were bathed and shaved and fed. For the first time in months, they were able to sleep knowing that they would make it through the next day. Yet they were changed. They hoarded food. They refused to be without rice. Many of the men were in such poor condition that they were deemed unfit for future military service, but others were fit, and on becoming aware that Wingate could be making a second larger raid, a number of the survivors volunteered.

To all intents and purposes, Operation LONGCLOTH was now over.

The officers, particularly the column commanders, had work to do. They had to collate intelligence and write it into reports. This included drawing up lists of the dead and missing. The figures made for grim reading: 3,000 men went in and 2,180 came out. Among the missing was Frank.

Lists were drawn up, witness statements taken and men and officers debriefed. Initial figures suggested that 450 men were known to have died during the expedition and 430 were either missing in action or were known to have been captured. Many of those who were missing had been left behind or separated and had either died of disease, exhaustion, wounds or were murdered, either by Burmese bandits or the enemy.

Some 246 British Chindits and 120 Gurkhas were recorded as prisoners of war by the Japanese. The records contain only those who reached the PoW camps. The actual number captured was higher, but some died or were killed en route. Of those who were taken prisoner, only two-fifths would see their homes again. For Frank, now with his hands bound and bayonets pointing at him, the odds were bad.

For those who had made it out however, their exploits were now headline news. On 20 May, Wingate held a press conference and declared the mission a success. *The Times* newspaper headline ran as follows:

THREE MONTHS IN ENEMY COUNTRY
from our Special Correspondent, G.H.Q., India May 20

One of the best-kept secrets of the war is disclosed in an official announcement today that a long-range jungle force led by Brigadier Orde Charles Wingate of Abyssinian fame, and supported entirely by air, has come out of northern Burma after spending three months as wreckers in the midst of this wild, enemy-controlled territory.

Operating in several columns – three of them British and the others Gurkha, with detachments of Burma Rifles serving the purposes of intelligence and reconnaissance – the Wingate brigade penetrated more than 300 miles across the jungle ranges and valleys; two big, swift rivers, the Chindwin and Irrawaddy, were crossed, and among other achievements the Myitkyina railway was cut in as many as 80 places in the general region of Katha. By that time the force had drawn upon itself the best part of a Japanese division, thus undoubtedly relieving the enemy's pressure on the Chinese in Yunnan, and many a running engagement was fought before and after the decision was wisely taken to withdraw.

A hotly debated topic followed, and has been argued by academics and military historians for decades after: what did the expedition achieve? The Chindits had gone hundreds of miles behind enemy lines. They had fought many times their number and the sheer number of enemy dead lay as proof that the Japanese soldiers were not unbeatable. They had destroyed communication lines, railways and bridges. Huge numbers of Japanese troops had to be diverted from other operations to hunt the raiders. For a small force, their achievements were admirable.

Many critics felt that nothing tangible was gained. This is true to a point: no land was retaken, though that was not the aim of the raid. The railways had been destroyed, but they could be fixed. Many enemy were killed and thousands of Japanese troops had to be diverted to try to track down the elusive and deadly British force. However, the Japanese had no shortage of troops – an army of more than 300,000 in Burma – and the Chindits did not make much of a dent in the Japanese force.

Many of the critics failed to understand the point of the operation. This was the first testing of a long-range penetration force, deployed behind enemy lines and re-supplied by air. It proved that well-trained men could work effectively to damage and harass an enemy and could do so in small mobile groups. Above all, the men of LONGCLOTH as they blazed their trail through the jungles, hills and rivers of Burma were able to gain valuable information so that when the Chindits of Operation THURSDAY followed in 1944, they went armed with knowledge, intelligence and improved methods.

It was crude and many errors were made, but Wingate proved it could work and the men who followed him planted the seeds from which the idea and methods of elite Special Forces would grow.

* * *

Behind the glare of publicity, somewhere in an army office in England, a typist filled in yet another template letter, this one addressed to Mrs Sarah Berkovitch of 32 Greenstead Avenue, undated. It was placed before an officer of the Records Department in a pile with the rest to be signed.

My great-grandmother had not had an easy life. With her husband Louis, they had moved from Romania to escape rampant anti-Semitism and anti-Jewish decrees. A mother of nine children, they arrived penniless in England and lived in poverty, with Louis working as a tailor's presser. One of her sons, Jack, had become involved in low-level criminality and had fallen foul of a gang over some stolen goods he had been handling. They sought him out and murdered him, hitting him over the head with a cosh in the street. Her husband was by then confined to a secure mental hospital where he remained until he died thirty-one years later. Her other sons were all away in the army.

The telegram would have been delivered by a postman. She would have come to the door and been handed an official envelope; the knock every parent dreaded. No good news would be in that letter and she would have known it. Was she able to stand? She opened it with shaking hands: 'Madam, I regret to have to inform you that a report has been received from the War Office...'

Were any of her daughters there as she collapsed to the floor on reading the first line? The letter continued:

...to the effect that No. 3780027 Private Berkovitch, F., Regiment 13th Bn. was posted as 'missing' on the date not yet known in the Indian Theatre of War.

The report that he is missing does not necessarily mean that he has been killed, as he may be a prisoner of war or temporarily separated from his regiment.

Official reports that men are prisoners of war take some time to reach this country, and if he has been captured by the enemy it is probable that unofficial news will reach you first...

'Missing', not dead. 'Missing.' Possibly alive? Surely alive? Missing, maybe just lost. Was a friend with her now? A daughter? Someone to calm her down? 'Look Sarah, it says "He may be a prisoner of war or temporarily separated from his regiment." He will be okay.'

Had she heard rumours of the appalling treatment of prisoners of war by the Japanese? The best she could now hope for was that her son was in their hands. The telegram is undated. She would have received it before 22 July 1943. On that date, the *Manchester Evening News* ran a story titled '"Silent" Man with Wingate', which reads as follows:

Pte Frank Berkovitch of Greenstead Avenue, Crumpsall, never told his mother that he was a member of the now-famous Wingate Expedition into the Burma Interior. But another soldier's mother gave the news to Mrs Berkovitch. Now Private Berkovitch has been posted missing in the Indian theatre of war. He is officially attached to the Gurkha Rifles.

By the time this reached the press, Frank, who for me too was a silent man, had been a prisoner of the Japanese for three months.

In desperation, Sarah began to write letters. She did not give up, and at some point wrote directly to Wingate. On 10 November 1943, she received a reply from Headquarters, Special Force, c/o India Command. The letter was from Major General Wingate:

Dear Mrs Berkovitch,

I will take steps to see whether I can find out anything further about your son. You must not allow your anxiety to make you ill. You say your son was your main support. In that case, until you receive news of him, I hope you will allow me to fill his place in this respect. Please let me know what you need and regard it as a gift gladly made in honour of my friend Berkovitch. In the meantime, I sincerely hope I can get some good news for you.

For news as to your son's whereabouts, if a prisoner of war in Japanese hands, you should apply to the British Red Cross. They may or may not be able to get the information, but they do obtain news of a large proportion of prisoners, usually after many months delay.

Yours sincerely, Major-General O. Wingate

At the time Wingate wrote the letter, he was working long hours, engaged in the huge administrative task of building a much larger force for the second Chindit raid into Burma. He sat at his desk with the letter from Sarah and took time to dictate a reply; a reply in which he called Frank not a soldier, not a private, not his batman, but his friend.

103

Chapter Eight

'The caged bird sings with a fearful trill, of things unknown, but longed for still, and his tune is heard on the distant hill, for the caged bird sings of freedom.'

Caged Bird, Maya Angelou

As his sergeant fell down dead and those around him cried out from the pain of bullet wounds and Japanese soldiers were shouting and kicking, bayonets jabbing with rifle barrels trained on him, Frank's entire world condensed into those few seconds, his entire consciousness focused on whether this was the end or there was any way out. Weapons dropped – hands up – a shove to the ground, a strike with a rifle butt: 'They tied our hands behind our backs and took all our possessions. They then marched us to a camp called Hintha, then started to interrogate us, but there was little that we could tell them.'

As they were marched off, Frank may have felt a glimmer of hope. Surely, he may have thought, if he was to be killed, this would have been done straight away. News of the cruel deaths of two other Chindits, Menzies and Gilmartin, tied to trees and tortured, had reached the other columns and they all knew of the wounded Royal Marine Commandos who were taken prisoner during the general retreat, while covering the retreat as the rearguard the year before and who had been used as live targets for bayonet practice.

Captured men were usually interrogated soon after they were caught. It was here that Frank's rank as a private would have helped. In the Imperial Army, a private was given very little information and as such the Japanese captors tended to assume that British privates did not know much. That would not stop them being beaten, but the beatings were not to extract information. The captors were wrong in their assumption as Wingate believed that all ranks should understand each aspect of the mission. Officers suffered far worse on capture, as Philip Stibbe was to discover. Told he would be shot or beheaded, he was beaten with bamboo sticks but refused to talk. Then water was forced down his throat to simulate drowning, and only then did he feign breaking down and used the opportunity to give false information to the enemy.[1]

From Twinnge, my grandfather and his wounded and doubtless terrified comrades were then moved on through the jungle. Did he think of escape? His kit taken, hands bound, no weapons, no food, his friends injured, and guarded by armed soldiers. Common sense would have told him that the odds of survival were negligible. 'The Japs then marched us, still with our hands tied behind our backs, to a place called Nampaung; they placed us in cages and made fun of us.'

It is hard to think of my grandfather in a cage. I imagine bamboo pens, lashed together with rope like in a Vietnam War film, with the captured men shoved in at gunpoint while immature, angry young men in uniforms mocked them. Frank's narrative continues:

Later, we were driven by lorry to a jail in Bhamo. In the jail we saw many more prisoners including Gurkhas. The sanitary conditions were awful with no medical facilities at all for the wounded. At night we lay on bare floorboards, the days seemed to drag on, but we rested at night.

The treatment of the prisoners worsened as they moved further away from the areas where the fighting was taking place. Front-line soldiers such as those who ambushed Frank understood that they had a job to do, but those posted as prison guards – unfit for combat or paid civilian jailers – had a propensity towards cruelty. Frank sat behind the bars of the cells with sixty or so other men in them as the jailers mimed that the prisoners would be bayoneted. One of the Burmese jailers carried a steel golf club shaft and poked prisoners with it, until one of the Chindits took exception and attacked him.

On 12 May the prisoners were told that any fit men would be marched to Lashio and from there, they would be transported to Maymyo. The march would be 200 miles. Frank was on this march. The prisoners were warned that if anyone could not keep up, they would be shot. If anyone tried to escape, they would all be shot. They would be guarded on the way by a unit of mountain artillery soldiers who were making the same journey. Many of the prisoners had lost kit or their boots were worn out, so they were fitted out with spare bits of Japanese uniform.

The march was long, and as they climbed through hills the men were in a state of fatigue. It took two weeks. Frank described the journey:

We were then told to march once more. It was very hard for we were very weak from lack of food. The little rice and vegetables was not enough to give us the energy to carry on. We were in a shocking condition, but the threat of being shot if we fell out kept us moving; where we got the energy from to carry on, only God knows. We prayed while we marched because without God's help we would not have survived.

We were in a state of exhaustion, but we still carried on; the Japs put some of the worst cases on the ration lorries and the rest of us marched on into the Shweli Valley. By the time we arrived at Lashio we were in a very bad state.

Frank marched, bunched together with his weary comrades. Ragged and dejected, heads down under the rain, trudging through mud, praying as he walked, '*Baruch Shem K'Vod Malchuta L'Olam Va'ed*', his faith keeping him going. Also keeping him moving was the very real threat of a bullet. The kindness of strangers sustained him too. The people of Namkham had fared well under British rule, with the locals served by British missionaries and doctors who had set up schools and a hospital. They now suffered under Japanese occupation. As the men passed through Namkham, the locals handed the prisoners lumps of sugary jaggery, which must have seemed like manna from Heaven.[2] Eventually, the wretched procession reached Lashio and Frank and the other prisoners were transported from there to the next camp: 'We were herded into cattle trucks and sent on our way to Maymyo.'

The cattle trucks into which Frank and the other captives were transported were railway carts designed for about four cows. Into each, in the sweltering heat and humidity of the monsoon season, more than twenty-five men were crammed and the trains headed into the hill town of Maymyo, 25 miles to the east of Mandalay.

Maymyo, meaning May's Town, was named after Colonel May, a British commander who had been stationed there in the late nineteenth century, was renamed Pyin Oo Lwin by the Myanmar military junta. It was where, just a couple of years earlier, Mike Calvert had run the Bush Warfare School and was a popular retreat for British officers and their families. Houses and administrative buildings had been built in British Colonial style, centred around a large botanical garden, and it was, for a time, a fashionable part of the Empire. For the captured men, it was a place of viciousness that would haunt its survivors throughout their lives. Frank wrote in his memoir:

We hoped that when we arrived there the Japs would treat us a little better, but it was not to be. The guards carried clubs, which they were very fond of using on the prisoners for the slightest reason.

I saw a pal (of mine) hit by the Japs and then kicked in the shins till he couldn't walk; it was like being on the edge of a volcano. The treatment in the camp was really rough and very painful at times. They would beat us when we did not bow to the sentry in the camp. Then more prisoners were brought into the camp and dysentery broke out, but the Japs did not help us and conditions deteriorated and lots of our boys died.

All who endured Maymyo were united in the view that it was brutal, the guards malevolent and the atrocities committed unforgivable. It was essentially a transit camp to where the increasing numbers of captured men could be brought before being moved on to Rangoon Jail. It served another purpose, though, as a disciplinary camp. This was where prisoners were 'taught' to accept and understand Japanese discipline, to learn Japanese commands and to have it beaten into them that they were no longer soldiers but prisoners who had taken the route of surrender, so shameful in *bushido* that they were beneath contempt.

The guards were the dregs of the Imperial Army, third-rate soldiers gifted with almost unbridled power to act with ruthless cruelty. The Korean guards, working under the Japanese, were considered to be even worse than their overlords: Take people like that and give them a club and tell them to use it, and they will do so with pleasure.

Prisoners were regularly taken away for interrogation and would come back battered and bruised. Daily, Frank stood in a line. He stood and waited his turn as each day the men were lined up to have their faces slapped by guards as a ritual humiliation. Daily, my grandfather would steel himself and wait his turn as a malicious, craven guard, who would be inconsequential in any time of peace, made his way along the line. When the guard reached him, did Frank look down at his feet or did he have enough defiance left in him to hold the gaze of his assailant? Maybe at first, or if not Frank, maybe others did not capitulate, but after being thrashed and attacked day after day, the resilience of even the most insolent of the captured Chindits started to break.

When a guard was having a bad day or felt more than their usual animosity to a prisoner, they would swap the slap for a punch or kick to the shins, or they would knock the prisoner down with the butt of a rifle or club. Failing to stand to attention while this went on made it worse, and hitting back could be fatal.

Each day, the men were taken out in working parties as slave labour. British bombing raids often targeted Maymyo, so Frank and his comrade prisoners would dig air-raid shelters under armed guard and rip down bombed-out buildings.

The food was insufficient; rice and vegetables with just the occasional small piece of meat or fish. The labour was hard and heavy and the men had already lost body weight during their campaign before capture. They were now seriously malnourished. Furthermore, there was no medical assistance. The local Burmese, though, were pro-British and did what they could to ease the plight of the prisoners, bringing food to the work parties.

Exhausted from digging trenches and moving rubble, the men would come back into the camp and take part in drill parade. The prisoners were taught to number off in Japanese for the regular roll-calls, to bow low every time a guard walked past or entered a room. Slapped, kicked, beaten with clubs and rifle butts, the prisoners learned the drill very quickly. The salutes had to be snappy and smart, the bows low. Any shortfall would lead to a severe beating: 'They would beat us when we did not bow to the sentry in the camp.' How many times was Frank clubbed to the ground, trying to protect his head as blows rained down?

Each day, morning and evening, the prisoners would attend the 'Toots Parade'. It was a religious Shinto prayer ceremony. The nickname was given to it because the responses of the Japanese guards to some of the prayers sounded like 'Toots'. As the guards bowed towards Japan, the prisoners were expected to bow, and any slight sign of disrespect was met with violence.

The living arrangements were small wooden huts, the size of a bathing hut or tool shed, with four to six men sleeping in each one, plagued by mosquitos. Filthy and without sanitary arrangements or running water, dysentery broke out and more lives were lost. Nobody knows how many died in Maymyo; Frank simply said 'lots of our boys died'. Some were already wounded or very ill and did not last long.

At The National Archives, there is a file numbered WO361436 which contains an extraordinary document. It is a report containing a subheading 'Extract from Kachin Levies Intelligence Report, number 56, for week ending 11 December 1943' and reads as follows:

During the period two escaped POWs have arrived, one of whom brought in a valuable collection of Jap propaganda which is enclosed with this summary. Other general information from these men is as follows:

The 77th Bde POWs in MAYMYO were kept in the servants' quarters east of the Railway Station. These buildings are just across from the old 'Bush Warfare School'. Treatment in this jail is bad and 5 B.O.Rs. (British Other Ranks) have died: names not known.

Maymyo had an even darker side. Among the atrocities committed by Japan were medical experiments carried out on prisoners of war. These had started before the Second World War. During the years of occupation in China, Lieutenant Shiro Ishii set up and ran Unit 731, a military research unit that carried out experiments on prisoners of war. The experiments included vivisection of live prisoners, infection with pathogens and poisons and barbaric tests to determine how long a person could be frozen or subjected to pressure. Some 3,000 prisoners were murdered in these experiments.

Experiments were also committed on Allied soldiers during the war. The victims included Chindits held at Maymyo and Kalaw. A group of prisoners moved from Maymyo to Rangoon Jail arrived in an awful condition and most died soon after arrival. They had been injected with malaria germs.[3]

After the war, in a shameful engagement in realpolitik, General MacArthur worked to obtain immunity for the perpetrators of medical experiments in exchange for the data they had collated. Shiro Ishii was never prosecuted and, after the war, advised the United States on development of bio-weapons.

At Maymyo Frank was beaten, starved and used as slave labour, but was fortunate to survive. He talks of the treatment being very painful at times. The assaults were probably with clubs. I think about the fear he would have felt as it was clear a guard was coming towards him, the relief when the guard stopped raining blows on him, of the helplessness when his friends were assaulted and the anger and grief when men died. Yet I know that luck, only luck – good for him, bad for others – meant that he was not one of the ones picked at random from a list and marked for atrocious and perverse human experiments from which he would have died.

* * *

There is, as I write this and during the many times I have thought of Maymyo, a burning anger in me that will not subside. Although I doubt the perpetrators would have ever felt regret or reflected in any depth on their crimes, should they have done, there is no forgiveness in me for what they did to Frank and to the others. My honest feelings towards his tormentors are of hatred. It was with thoughts of what Frank had endured, and of those who were murdered or allowed to die by act or omission, and of the experiments and the degradation, that I travelled the road to Pyin Oo Lwin.

The scenery, as we ascended the 1,000ft to the town, was charming and the huts and fields from the road leading to the hill gave way to large houses and well-tended gardens. Clearly it remains an affluent area. Many of these houses are now in the hands of the military elite, with their officers stationed at the base in the town.

Stopping at a roadside café, the proprietor asked why I was there. She brought me tea and a samosa as I told her the reason for my journey. With a warm smile, she told me she had something to show me. After rummaging in a cabinet, she produced a transparent plastic wallet. Inserted neatly were rows of the Japanese paper currency that had been paid to Burmese traders. She had collected them simply out of interest and as a piece of local history and was glad of the opportunity to be able to show a clearly fascinated visitor. She explained that some Burmese acquired a lot of this money from trading with the Japanese – they had little choice as this was how the Japanese paid – but this profit was literally 'on paper' and any true value was predicated on

Japan winning the war. Following the defeat of the Imperial Army, the currency became worthless and was simply thrown away.

I was journeying to the railway station. My clue to the location of where the prisoners had been held was based on the report of the two escapees in the 'Extract from Kachin Levies Intelligence Report': 'The 77th Bde POWs in MAYMYO were kept in the servants' quarters east of the Railway.'

I arrived at the railway station, the very same railway station where the cattle trucks had arrived after a whole day of travel with their human cargos and where Frank and the other prisoners were then taken to Maymyo prison camp. The railway station is a single-storey, red-brick building with a corrugated iron roof. A loudspeaker is tethered above the entrance and the announcements come through in a distorted crackle.

The station master agreed to see me and gestured for me to take a seat inside his cream-painted office among old wooden cupboards where he sat with his assistant. Neat stacks of cash and handwritten ledger books were laid out before them. Both men looked to be about 50, clean-shaven and smart, in neatly-pressed white shirts with name badges. Behind them was a blue poster taped to the wall showing ticket prices, with destinations written in English and Burmese. One of the destinations was Lashio, from where Frank had been transported at the end of the gruelling march of 200 miles from Bhamo Jail.

The station master was confident about where the old staff quarters were; he pointed me across the tracks to three large buildings on the east side. I could reach them over the tracks. The easiest way was to climb onto the platform and down onto and over the track. The buildings were down a pathway opposite the platform. On the platform, a young man with a prosthetic leg lay sleeping on a bench. His wife sat by him begging for money and another family, further along, sat on the floor among sacks and baskets of vegetables. An elderly lady with a weathered face beneath a straw hat sat surrounded by large sacks of purple and yellow flowers and was wrapping them into bunches with newspaper, destined as offerings at pagodas from her customers.

I climbed down from the platform and onto the narrow-gauge tracks. The pathway described by the station master was straight ahead. A fence ran along the side of the railway line but stopped on both sides of the track. I walked over the tracks towards the path, passing a family of five in flip-flops and *lunghis*, with the only lady in the procession leading the way with a large filled white sack balanced on her head. Immediately to my right on the path were two red-brick, teak-framed houses with corrugated iron roofs and teak balconies jutting out of the front and back of them. The houses were set apart from each other in a large, untended garden. Further down the track was a dirt-stained, white concrete house.

I could see no evidence to say whether the red houses were occupied or not, but one was fenced off and the far one was locked up and seemed to be empty. I took photographs of the buildings and tried as best as I could to think through all that I had read. The prisoners were unlikely to have been housed in these buildings. Probably they were used by the Japanese officers, or possibly as barracks for guards or soldiers. The prisoners were locked in huts at night; several men in each mosquito-infested space with barely any room to lie down.

If I was in the right place, the huts were long gone and there was no trace left of them. I walked further down the track. The white house was being lived in; washing was hanging up but the teak door was closed and padlocked. I wandered up and down the track looking for any evidence of the huts, barbed wire fences, watch towers; I don't know why I expected to see any of this. If I am honest with myself, I was quite glad I didn't. I felt uncomfortable. Somewhere in this area, very close to where I was walking, at night-time, my grandfather was sleeping in a cramped hut with other men and getting what little rest they could before the next day of beatings, humiliation and forced labour. What happened here had occupied my thoughts in the lead-up to my trip and my imagination was playing out the scenes I had read about like an old war film on repeat. I did not want to see the huts and to step inside. I would have done. I would have sat on the floor. I would have lain down to see if I could lie flat and if I could not have done, I would have thought of Frank, huddled up and unable to stretch out. I would have looked around and wondered how six men would fit, stretching out my arms to touch the walls.

There were no watch towers now. I could not see where the boundaries of the camp would have been, where the parades took place and the daily roll-calls. Maybe where I was standing, or certainly close to here, my grandfather would have stood in line, waiting for his turn to be slapped or clubbed. Very close to here, he saw his friend kicked in the shins until he couldn't walk, and close to here, prisoners of war were chosen and taken for medical experiments that they did not survive.

I felt irritated and on edge. I was angry at what had happened here. I was frustrated that there was not so much as a plaque to mark where the camp had stood. Of course there was not. What did I expect? A guidebook on sale at a neat museum shop? Guides with umbrellas aloft? There was nothing; no evidence whatsoever that seventy-four years earlier, hundreds of guards, soldiers and prisoners were here. Why should there be? What right did I have to expect the locals, who wanted neither British nor Japanese here, to commemorate the aggression and brutality of two Imperial forces who decided to have a scrap on their playground?

Chapter Nine

'You expected to be sad in the fall. Part of you died each year when the leaves fell from the trees and their branches were bare against the wind and the cold, wintery light. But you knew there would always be the spring, as you knew the river would flow again after it was frozen. When the cold rains kept on and killed the spring, it was as though a young person died for no reason.'

A Moveable Feast, Ernest Hemingway

Frank felt some relief when Japanese guards told the prisoners that all fit men were to be moved to Rangoon Jail. He did not believe a word they said when the guards told them there would be bread to eat and much better accommodation and even a weekly cinema showing. Yet all agreed that whatever Rangoon was going to be like, it could not be worse than what they were going through. Not that they had a choice, of course. Frank wrote of the journey:

> After many months there [Maymyo Camp] they started to move us to the railway, then placed us in cattle trucks with sentries to guard us. It was impossible to sit down with so many men in one truck, but at last we arrived at Rangoon Jail where they opened the gates and marched us into the compound.

Pressed together with the other prisoners in narrow cattle trucks, Frank stood sweating and sweltering under a corrugated iron roof, standing with no room to sit and taking turns to try to find a small space in which to sleep. The guards were between each carriage as the train rumbled along the narrow-gauge tracks. Three days later the train arrived in Rangoon Station. The men alighted and stared at the devastation wrought by bombing raids. Bombs had destroyed part of the station and surrounding buildings. Amid the ruins, the human cargo was assembled and marched through Rangoon, past the bright golden Shwedagon Pagoda, along a tree-lined road to the jail.

Rangoon Central Jail was large and imposing with huge stone walls and gates, built in a Victorian style with the prison blocks spreading outwards as spokes from a central hub which was a large water tower. The jail is now long gone, flattened during the time of military rule in Burma. I walked along the route Frank would have walked, past the gleaming Shwedagon Pagoda where the Buddhist faithful made their devotions, along a tree-lined avenue to where the jail once stood, now replaced with a hospital and surrounded by the numerous shops and roadside stalls that pop up wherever there is space in the growing city.

Tired and nervous, Frank waited his turn to be searched and then, together, they were ordered and shoved through the gates and into a courtyard: 'We found lots of our men from the Brigade in the camp; also many officers.'

As Frank entered the courtyard with the other prisoners from Maymyo, other Chindit prisoners, already in the courtyard, approached them. A moment of hesitation, and then recognition. Hands were shaken, news exchanged, questions asked: 'Did you make it over the Irrawaddy?', 'Any news of the Brigadier?', 'So glad to see you alive but wish it could have been in India', 'What are we in for here?', 'Is there food?', 'We need medicines.' There was some relief in that first evening among the new arrivals that they were at least together, with friends they could count on.

Frank was placed in Block 6. The jail was split with the Indians in one block, Chinese prisoners in another and the other blocks divided between the British soldiers and American airmen. The Chindits from Maymyo were spared a period in solitary confinement and the brutal induction and interrogations faced by some officers and by the US airmen at the New Law Courts at the hands of the dreaded *Kempeitai*, the Japanese Secret Police.

Block 6 held about 120 prisoners and the majority of the Chindits were imprisoned in this block. The total number of Chindits held in Rangoon Central Jail during the war from both Chindit expeditions was approximately 210. Others had died before reaching Rangoon. Of those who entered Rangoon, in excess of 60 per cent would die there. The odds on Frank's survival were now heavily stacked against him.

The block was a long building with wooden bars down one side, separating it from the corridor running alongside, down which guards would patrol when the men were locked up. Along the other side were glassless, barred windows. The ground floor where Frank, as a private, would now live for more than a year and a half had a concrete floor, with a wooden floor above where the officers would live. There was no improvement in conditions for the officers; they were simply separated from the other ranks. Each floor was split into five rooms. After a period of time, sick and injured men were moved from Block 3 to Block 6 and three of the rooms were used as makeshift hospitals. This meant that there were about forty men living in each of the other two rooms. During the period when the prison had been under British administration, the maximum capacity allowed was twenty-eight.[1] The cells, despite best efforts to keep them clean, remained infested with vermin and fleas.

The compound held a large water trough for washing and, at the other end, latrines. There was no running water and the toilets were simply ammunition tins or metal barrels to be emptied by hand. There was no disinfectant. They leaked. They attracted flies. The flies brought disease. The guards proved too foolish and stubborn to listen to the pleas of prisoners to improve the conditions, even when it was explained to them that flies are indiscriminate as to whom they transmit disease. The beds were wooden platforms or the floor. Blankets became infested with lice and germs and when the monsoon rains came, disease increased and so did death rates.

The days became a harsh routine. Each day would start and end with *Tenko*, the roll-call. The prisoners would form up ready for the arrival of the Japanese guards. Frank's number was Prisoner 306 *San Rei Roku* and twice a day, he would call it out:

> …life in the jail was very bad. Roll-call took place morning and night; we had to fall in on parade and with the words of command in Japanese we were called to attention, then gave our (PoW) number in Japanese. Numbers like *Ichi-nee-san-go*, then eyes right and then bow. You got beat up if you did not bow to them and we worked like slaves.

The guards served under a sadistic commandant, First Lieutenant Koshima. Any attempt at escape, it was made clear, would carry a penalty of death.

Maymyo had at least prepared the men for what to expect. Frank knew his salutes must be smart and snappy, that he must bow immediately as the sentry approached. He knew that if he did not, he would be punched, kicked or receive a blow from a club or a rifle butt. He learned quickly too, that even if he did everything right, a perceived mistake or sign of disrespect from another prisoner would result in group punishments and that this happened daily.[2] In the other British block, the commandant singled out Brigadier Hobson, the ranking British officer in the prison, captured at the fall of Singapore, and regularly Koshima would beat him with a steel-shafted golf club.

'We worked like slaves…' Frank and the other prisoners, officers included, would be sent out of the camp each day under armed guard as work details. Escape may have been on the minds of some, but there was nowhere to go, the risk of betrayal was significant, the Japanese occupied the whole area and the spectre of beheading if caught and of collective punishments against the other men was too high. There was only one tragic escape. One of the men who had been experimented on at Maymyo was in a delirious state and somehow managed to get out. He was brought back to the Japanese by Burmans and was taken away and killed.[3]

Much of the work was at the docks, loading and unloading boats and railways carts. The Chindits in captivity were beaten, but not entirely broken. By nature, they were tough, unruly and insolent. They were prepared to take punishment for insubordination rather than fully submit. Their insolence turned into minor acts of sabotage: heavily dropping fuel barrels onto sharp stones to cause leaks, or 'accidentally' letting a crate of fuses for explosives fall into the water. These incidents needed to appear as genuine blunders or the reprisals would be severe. The punishments, when they took place on work details, were carried out in front of the native population as a policy of deliberate humiliation.[4]

As at Maymyo, the work assigned to work parties at Rangoon would include pulling down bombed-out buildings, digging air-raid shelters and building anti-aircraft installations. The air-raids were now regular and the docks were a target. Often the prisoners would need to dive for shelter as they heard the rumble of aircraft. Rangoon Central Jail itself was just a kilometre from the docks and there was nothing to mark it as a prisoner of war facility. The Red Cross had not been notified that prisoners were held there and from the air, the jail looked like warehouses or possibly barracks. It was enough to make it a target and as the months dragged on, the bombing raids increased, grating constantly on the nerves of the prisoners and the guards. Some of the bombs hit the mark and prisoners were killed, as was at least one guard.

It is a strange detail, however, that the Japanese captors did pay the prisoners for work. Payment was made due to an arcane requirement of their Shinto faith. In one of the few memories Frank shared of his time as a prisoner of war, I was young at the time and he was at my parents' house and was eating an egg. He said that when he was in the prison camp, he was paid enough to buy one egg a month. Then he said 'We gave all the eggs to the sick', and I remember him being very serious as he said it and then very quiet.

The pay, clearly, was a nominal sum, paid only for days worked and from which deductions were taken; it amounted to less than a dollar a month. The sick received no pay.[5] The money was pooled and what little items of food they could buy were shared among the men.

Aside from the hard labour to which Frank was subjected, he took on additional duties. Naturally, as a tailor, he was well suited to fix the ragged clothing worn by the prisoners. Trousers were all cut down into shorts to provide extra material. The Japanese had provided a small supply of needles and thread and occasionally some old rags and clothing. The men needed to appear dressed for roll-call and Frank, with a couple of men working under his tutelage as apprentice tailors, did what they could to provide some sort of uniforms. The heat of the day was usually oppressive. There was no need for clothing in the compound; that is to say there was no need for clothing to keep warm during the days, and the dignity of modesty had long since been abandoned as hopeless. The spare bits of material were used by Frank to manufacture loincloths for the men to go around in as basic underwear.[6]

The policy in the camp was a policy of sadism. It was a policy of humiliation through violence, fear and deprivation. The violence and fear were constant and the examples numerous. Men would be beaten with sticks and belts, and forced to stand under the baking sun holding planks above their heads. Groups of Burmese prisoners would be offered their freedom if they beat up prisoners. Colonel Power, who would eventually march out of the camp with Frank, was knocked unconscious in one of these gratuitous, grotesque displays.[7] Then there were the daily slaps and assaults by guards because prisoners did not jump to attention quickly enough. Guards had two types of boots: in their rubber boots they would sneak into the cells and then attack prisoners who had not heard them and jumped quickly enough to attention and then bowed, and with their steel toe-capped ammunition boots they would deliver sharp, bone-splitting kicks to the shins of prisoners. The attacks with split canes of bamboo were particularly dangerous because they would cut the skin and with such deplorable insanitary conditions, infection would often follow.

Most feared was solitary confinement in a 12ft x 14ft cell, filthy, with no window or sunlight, no washing facilities and no contact with other prisoners and, worst of all, no idea how long the confinement would last. One of the most appalling acts of cruelty under Commandant Koshima was to intentionally deprive the other prisoners of vital medical assistance by keeping two doctors who had been captured, Major Ramsay of the brigade column and Colonel MacKenzie, in solitary confinement for many weeks.

Each day, before and after work, Frank lined up with an improvised dish and a tin can, fashioned out of a piece of metal, for his allowance of food and ersatz tea. The food consisted of rice and an okra type of vegetable or dahl lentils. Occasionally, a small amount of fish or meat would be mixed in. Any eggs or fruit needed to be purchased from the meagre 'wages'. Daily, men were dying and the rations had to be supplemented. Frank and other men who were strong enough to be sent on work parties, in their compulsion to help their sick comrades, tried to smuggle any extra bits of food into the camp. They did this whenever they could and always at personal risk of violence:

> We lost a lot of wonderful men in the camp for the lack of good food. When we went out on work parties we would try to bring food from outside, but we got caught by the Japs and they beat us across our legs and face. We were losing a lot of men from the bad food; many died every day and you did not know if you were next.

Most of the men had already been infected with malaria and suffered dysentery. If they did not have it yet, they would do. Frank used to keep a bottle of quinine tablets in his room for the rest of his life to fight the recurring malaria that plagued him. He had dysentery too and survived it; doubled up with cramps and diarrhoea, dehydrated, expecting to die but, unlike many, pulling through. Frank wrote of the debilitating and painful beriberi. It results from malnutrition, or more specifically from a lack of thiamine. Affecting the circulatory system and ultimately the heart, it would start at the feet, and then the legs would swell up with liquid, getting higher up the body and eventually stopping the victim breathing:

> The disease that claimed a lot of men was beriberi. This disease attacked the men in the form of chronic diarrhoea, the man got thinner, whilst others swelled up from the feet upwards, working its way through the body, this caused fluid under the skin and they became inflated with water. About 70 per cent of the Wingate Brigade (that became PoWs) died in the camp.

The men became more and more emaciated as they slowly starved. 'You could see all of my ribs,' Frank once said. They gradually became skeletal, with sunken eyes, walking around in their loincloths.

The Japanese had a medical officer. Lieutenant Akio Onishi was prosecuted after the war by the British War Crimes Tribunal. He was sentenced to hang, but this was reduced to life imprisonment. Among his crimes had been the deliberate withholding of medicine from the prisoners. He was also suspected of injecting sick prisoners with various tropical diseases. Yet as much as his wicked behaviour caused death and suffering, so did his incompetence. He tried to operate on an American who had suffered an arm injury. The arm had already been amputated but a further operation was needed. Onishi operated, but at some point realized it was beyond his rudimentary ability and abandoned the operation. 'Such operations were supposed to be easy,' he pleaded in his statement to the War Crimes Tribunal.[8] 'Supposed' was a damning testimony to his ineptitude.

However, it was in this respect that the British medical officers shone. In a prison where courage and sense of duty among inmates were not in short supply, the medical officers were the heroes. Colonel MacKenzie and Major Ramsay took over the operation. With barely any equipment, they removed part of the arm, stopping the spread of gangrene. The patient survived the war.

In another case, American airmen had been pulled by their captain from their crashed bomber. They were badly burned and horrifically injured. At first they had been thrown into solitary, too severely burned to use their hands. Their faces were bandaged and for days they crawled on the floor trying to find any bits of food they could, or lay writhing in agony.[9] Dr MacKenzie and Dr Ramsay were able to eventually persuade the guards to allow them to take the three surviving injured men to Block 6. Their wounds were infested with maggots which needed to be pulled out with home-made tweezers. Two of the men had lost their eyes. Both of these men died, though the third man was saved and survived the war. The agony and screams of the dying men were heard by all the occupants of Block 6. Decades later, Leon Frank, in his audio testimony held at the Imperial War Museum remembered this.[10] As he starts to tell the story he is choking back tears. He recalled how they begged the Japanese for a gun to be able to put an end to the abject suffering of one of the men, a request that was refused. As he tells it, he is no longer holding back tears, he is crying. What memories would have made Frank cry, if he would have spoken about them out loud? What made him cry when he was alone?

Frank had little contact, if any, with MacKenzie, who was in Block 3. However, his admiration for Ramsay, who he assisted as an orderly in the makeshift hospital, remained undampened when he wrote his memoir decades later:

Those that had dysentery became so weak; I would not like to describe the filth and stench from the dysentery. When out on working parties the men got scratched or grazed on their legs and arms, which then developed into septic ulcers which slowly rotted the flesh away. Things got so bad they sent a Dr Ramsay to our part of the camp (Block 6).

He (Ramsay) got some medicines to help him; the men on working parties found some bluestones and brought them back into the camp and gave them to Dr Ramsay. He ground the bluestones and made them into a paste to put on the jungle ulcers. My word, he saved a lot of men, even though he was deprived of any drugs to work with, still he reduced the death rate in the camp.

The hospital in which Frank worked was of course not a hospital or anything close to one. He was called a 'veranda orderly'[11] because the hospital was just that: a wooden veranda in Block 6, leading onto the prison courtyard. A room in the block was also given over to the care of the sick and dying. Frank and the two or three other Chindits who served as orderlies did what they could to keep it clean, but it was like trying to hold back the tide. The washing facilities were minimal. Blankets and clothes were no sooner washed than the dysentery patients would soil them again with diarrhoea. Daily, Frank would help beriberi patients to the ammunition tins which served as latrines and through the days and nights, he and the other orderlies would empty and clean them out.

It was not a hospital: hospitals have dressings, drugs and instruments. There was none of that. A scalpel was fashioned from a razor blade fixed to a wooden handle; forceps had been made from bits of tin, and bandages were boiled strips of khaki uniform. Hospitals have medicines, but not here. Here the men had to beg for medicines. Ramsay was beaten up and thrown into solitary for demanding medicines and when medicines were handed over, it was never enough. Hospitals have nurses: here there were no nurses, just a handful of soldiers who wanted to keep their comrades alive. Frank lost many of his teeth in the prison. All the men did as a direct effect of malnutrition. Colonel MacKenzie, with no training and with the barest of hand-made equipment, had become the prison dentist.

The bluestones Frank wrote of were copper sulphate. Someone among the prisoners had the knowledge of what these bright blue crystals were and their application as a life-saving antiseptic:

There was a cholera outbreak in the camp (mid-June 1944) and Dr Ramsay risked his life looking after the sick. This was a terrible time for us, for you never knew who was going to be the next victim

126

of this disease. The Japanese were very worried for themselves and so Dr Ramsay was given medical supplies and drugs to help with the cholera disease and thank God the epidemic was checked, but not before many men died.

The outbreak was managed quickly by the camp doctors. The prisoners who contracted cholera were immediately isolated. The bamboo platforms they had been lying on and their clothing and blankets were burned and the room disinfected with lime chloride. The quick actions limited the deaths to about ten men. One of the men volunteered to look after the sick. He too died. Their bodies were immediately burned.

Starvation, disease, beatings, neglect. Men were dying daily. The Japanese allowed the dead to be buried in a nearby cemetery. There was no wood for coffins, but the prisoners wanted to ensure the dead had some dignity. No wood for coffins, but there were rice sacks. The bodies could be stitched into the rice sacks. That was the best that could be done, and the man who stitched the bodies into the rice sacks was Frank Berkovitch, the tailor.[12] Sometimes it would be one a day, sometimes more. On a good day, none at all.

Another prisoner, Ras Pagani, a serial escaper who had evaded the Germans at Dunkirk, slipped through the clutches of the Japanese at Singapore and escaped from the notorious Thai-Burma 'Death Railway' dressed as an Indian coolie, would prepare the bodies for burial, stuffing their orifices with rags to stop contagious bodily fluids leaking through the sacks. He never got over it.[13]

How many passed through their hands? As Frank, the last man to see the face of a dead comrade, a life gone which did not need to go, closed the sack, folded it over and let his hands deftly and expertly work his needle and thread, he mumbled a quiet prayer. Were these the faces that came back to him in the nightmares from which he suffered for the rest of his days?

Once again, his faith sustained Frank. It is easy to be dismissive of this suggestion, putting his survival down to physiological factors and sheer luck, but in a living hell such as Rangoon, as friends died daily, as Japanese clubs and rifle butts rained down, many men lost hope and gave up. From then on, it was a rapid decline. Yet Frank's faith gave him some inner strength and that was some advantage in arresting his despair and decline. As he prayed, it brought a few moments of peace. He would pray daily in the prison, with the small soldier's prayer book he had carried through the whole ordeal – actually no, it carried him – and finding a quiet corner as he intoned the ancient blessings: 'May He who makes peace in Heaven, make peace for us all…' Always respected for his beliefs, an officer would tell the men to be quiet when they became too loud: 'Quiet everybody, a man is saying his prayers.'[14]

* * *

Just over one year later, on 24 March 1944, during Operation THURSDAY, Orde Wingate was killed when the B-25 Mitchell bomber in which he was travelling crashed close to the village of Thuilon in the Tamenglong District of Manipur State, India after setting off from a fortified Chindit base in Burma named Broadway.

Churchill said of him in a letter to Wingate's widow Lorna: 'I had recognized him as a man of genius, who might well have become also a man of destiny.'[15]

If the best assessment of a person's ability is what is thought of them by their enemy, Lieutenant General Mutaguchi, on hearing of Wingate's death, recalled his reaction: 'I realized what a loss this was to the British army and said a prayer for the soul of this man in whom I had found my match.'[16]

News usually reached the men in Rangoon as new captives brought in word from the front or bits of information were collected from local Burmese when the prisoners went out on work parties. On this occasion, the news of Wingate's death came directly from the guards who ran through the jail waving the *Greater Asia* newspaper, shouting '*Wingate shinde, Wingate shinde.*' I have no doubt it hit many of the Chindits hard. Although some were bitter about some of the decisions he had made, he was still their visionary leader, the man who had believed in them, built them into warriors and pushed them to take the fight to the Japanese. For Frank, who as his batman had perhaps spent more time with him than any other private in the expedition, the loss was profound.

Other news began to come through. The Allies were advancing. The Fourteenth Army was pushing back the Japanese forces. As 1944 drew to a close, the men and the guards did not need to be told about the increased bombing raids or the shift in air superiority towards the Allies. The guards were too fearful now to take out working parties as the docks were targeted. Frank, with the prisoners, looked up from the compound as formations of US bombers, including the new powerful B-29s, flew above them; their feelings of fear that they would be hit evaporating and being replaced with elation when the planes passed on and explosions and smoke rose from some unseen target. The war had turned, and slowly, the prisoners began to believe that there may be an end in sight.

Yet there was a nervousness too. Rumours circulated that the Japanese guards had received a 'Kill All' command, ordering that all prisoners should be killed rather than fall into Allied hands. Certainly these orders had been given to many PoW commandants in other camps and some would be carried out. In the Philippines, following flawed intelligence that Allied forces were about to land on the island of Palawan, prisoners of war who were being held there were herded into air-raid shelters that were set on fire, with any who escaped being machine-gunned.

The guards began to behave differently. Their brutality towards airmen increased as the bombings grew in frequency, but as the spring of 1945 approached, they became more nervous. Some of the guards began to ask prisoners what would happen to them if the Americans arrived.[17] The sounds of advancing infantry started to come closer and Frank's time in Rangoon Jail was coming to its end.

Chapter Ten

'Go, tell the Spartans, passerby,
that here by Spartan law we lie.'

Simonedes of Ceos

The guards were in disarray and behaving erratically. One afternoon, amid the carnage around the jail, they spent an hour practising bowing to each other.[1] Food rations had started to improve too. Allied fighter planes now completely dominated the skies, artillery could be heard and news filtered through that the Burmese Defence Army had started to rebel against the Japanese. It was clear that the end was imminent. General Slim and the men of the Fourteenth Army had taken Central Burma. Operation DRACULA had commenced to retake Rangoon. Gurkha and Indian regiments secured key airfields and blocked off the Rangoon River, creating beachheads to land supplies, artillery and infantry. Japanese commanders in Rangoon were ordered to defend it to the last man but defied their orders, moving their troops to Pegu and Moulmein.

On 24 April, the guards began burning records. The largest supply yet of vegetables, together with four water buffalo for slaughter, was brought into the compound. For the first time, the men were able to eat until they were full.

On the morning of the following day, *Tenko* was held as normal. The guards, fidgety, were scurrying around afterwards preparing kit, but clearly in a state of confusion. The men, whose sense of humour had survived the horrors they had faced, had assigned nicknames to the guards: the Ape, Funny Face, Pompous Percy, the Jockey, the Kicker, which now seemed more apt than ever.

Brigadier Hobson, the ranking British officer was summoned to the commandant. An order was given that all men who were able to walk were to be marched out of the camp. There were arguments with the guards about which men were fit enough to go. The prisoners knew the Allies were close, so close. What would happen to the sick? Who would care for them? Left alone in the jail they could be killed as soon as the healthier men were removed. Speculation was rife; some men preferred to stay and wait it out while others felt safer leaving. Officers needed to work through lists and talk to the men to decide who would go and who would stay.[2] The commandant eventually ordered just over 400 men to leave the prison. The intention was to move them towards Thailand for use as labour and as hostages. The Japanese still held the area of Pegu to the north-east of Rangoon, where fanatical troops were dug in for a last stand. Just two weeks before the monsoon storms were due to arrive, making roads impassable, the men were to be marched to Pegu over the Sittang bridge, about 180 miles away, towards Thailand.

The 400 men chosen to go were issued with some Japanese army clothing and a supply of rations. Some were assigned to push carts containing ammunition and supplies. A warning was given that any man caught trying to escape would be beheaded.[3] Flanked by Japanese guards with rifles and fixed bayonets, the motley column formed up, with Colonel Hobson standing tall at the front of the group, and the 'Pegu Marchers' walked out of Rangoon Jail. Among them was Frank:

Finally, about midday on 25 April (1945), we were told that all fit men, both British and American prisoners, would be leaving for an unknown destination. At this hour the Japs produced large amounts of food for us on the long march. We all felt that all our hopes for an early release were shattered and we would possibly be shot before our troops arrived in Rangoon. The wounded and sick stayed in the camp with a few guards and we hoped they would be ok.

The men straggled along, some in loincloths, some partly clothed in Japanese uniforms. The roads were difficult to walk along. Refugees, elephants and buffalo had churned them up and frequently there were large craters where bombs had exploded. The uneven surface made walking even more painful. Several times they had to dive for cover as Allied planes flew in low to attack. As it became clear that it was too dangerous to march by day, they continued at night. Describing the forced march, Frank wrote:

> I can only describe the pathetic sight: some of us had home-made sandals, but most of us in bare feet, we marched all day, we were exhausted and footsore. We rested for a short time in an area subjected to bombing as we were near Prome Airfields. It was not safe to move by day; at nightfall we marched to a junction near the Prome Road and then marched through paddy fields and by a village near Pegu. One officer took ill and we never saw him again, probably the Japs shot him. We marched again at night; many more fell out of the march and were never seen again.
>
> We were resting at the side of the road when we heard aircraft overhead, then we heard heavy explosions from the area of Rangoon and were worried about our lads back in the camp. We then pressed on towards Pegu; we could see the glow in the sky not far from Rangoon. Our feet were very sore and it was agony to march. Words cannot convey the mental torture we were going through; the rest was a prolonged torture we were going through in aching bodies.

The officer was most likely to have been Arthur Best. I looked for his resting-place at the Taukkyan War Cemetery. I looked down the lists of names, so many names, laid out in small print in the volumes of books in which the dead are detailed, but he has no marked grave. It is possible he lies in one of the hundreds of unknown graves marked simply as 'Known Unto God'. His name, like Sergeant Burrows, is simply engraved on one of the memorial columns, again too high to touch.

The men had now gone for forty-eight hours without food and their water supply had now run out too. Already starved and skeletal, all suffering from some disease, they were all close to the end, all close to collapse and death from exhaustion or a Japanese bayonet or bullet. Where they could they helped men along, cajoling and pleading with them to keep moving. Colonel MacKenzie, whose skill and courage had kept so many alive, could go no further and he told the men to leave him, but then two men came up and with their remaining strength took his arms over their shoulders and supported his emaciated body. As their strength failed, two more took over. After each stop, two men were at his side to keep him moving.[4]

The Japs were in a very awkward predicament, with our troops moving in and the Japs trying to get out with the prisoners to a safe place. We did not know where they were taking us; suddenly our planes came overhead during the day and fired their guns as they swooped down on us, being very suspicious of our movements. Words cannot convey the nervous strain put on us, for to be machine-gunned from our planes would be the last straw.

They must have thought we were Japs and we were lucky very few were wounded and killed from the machine-gun bullets and cannon fire. We spent the rest of the day hiding in a nearby wood and thinking about the possibilities of escaping, but wondered what chance we would have with the attitude of the Burmese towards us, for they were all for the Japs.

I drove along the road towards Pegu. The woods are still there along part of it; teak trees, fenced off for their value. The road along which Frank walked, where he scrambled for cover, pressing himself to the ground as they were strafed by their own planes, is now a large, busy tarmac road lined with shops. Here, so near to where I was walking, Frank's fight to survive was coming to its finale. He marched onwards, willing one foot in front of another and refusing to give up:

We marched on; everything seemed like a crazy dream. We were weary and footsore and some of the men could not carry on any further; the Colonel told the Japs that the men could not march any more and persuaded the guards to let us rest in the woods. The cooks were busy getting some food and hot drinks for the men and the Japs let us rest up for the rest of the day. Suddenly, someone shouted out for us to pay attention while Colonel Power made an announcement.

We all turned towards our Colonel; we did not dream what was coming next. Then we heard in a clear voice that everybody could hear that we were all free men. There was an audible gasp from the men, and then some were weeping and laughing, we went crazy with joy, shaking and hugging each other. The Japs had left us; we were advised to stay where we were as our own troops were advancing from the north. However, we were caught up with the Japs trying to get out of Burma and our troops coming in fast; we found ourselves in a very bad spot; we were free, but in great fear.

When some semblance of order was restored we decided we would try and make contact with our own troops. Using all available white clothing and some help from the Burmese, who had now turned on the Japs, I made a Union Jack in record time and laid it out in the paddy field. We hoped that this would show that we were British prisoners of war, just released by the Japanese and they would send us food, a wireless transmitter and medical supplies.

As Frank was making a flag, some men began to forage for food, approaching nearby villages. Other men were using blankets from the carts to spell out an SOS message:

We then heard shelling bombardments in the distance, it must be our troops advancing, then several planes came over very low and must have seen our message and reported back to Headquarters. From what we were told later on, they thought it impossible that we were prisoners of war and thought it was a Japanese trick they were pulling. So the planes came back and bombed and machine-gunned us as we hid behind some large trees.

Several men clung together in deep holes trying to protect ourselves as the planes came back again and again. At last the planes returned to base; a lot of men were killed, but we could not blame our airmen for they thought we were Japs. How could they know that 400 British and Americans had suddenly appeared out of the blue in no man's land? They assumed we were Japs; it was very cruel that anyone should have been killed during his first hour of freedom and the tragedy hung over us all.

One officer was killed. It was Brigadier Hobson, the senior officer in Rangoon Jail, the man who was beaten and humiliated by the malicious Commandant Koshima for pleading for better treatment for his men. The man who had marched out of the jail with my grandfather, at the head of the column, was killed by his own side in his first moments of freedom:

Our one objective was to get away before the accursed planes returned; we moved back over the paddy fields into a village. The Headman of the village said that there were still Japs around, but the Burmese were hunting them down. This was soon confirmed when rifle fire was heard not far from us. It was very important we try and contact our troops so a Burmese guide and Major Lutz went to try and make contact. They started out up a gentle slope, when suddenly out of the darkness a tense command rang out, our American Major replied and we then knew we were safe.

Figures appeared from the darkness and grasped us by the hands; we moved in a kind of dream, the officer in charge of the patrol told us not to worry as his men would take good care of us. We were told to keep our heads down as there was still firing going on, they then told us that the war was over back home and that the war would not last long in Burma for our lads were moving fast through the country.

We were thrilled to be free again after all the horrors we had been through and in a kind of dream. We moved on and came to some lorries waiting for us out and away from the Japs and toward our lines. One hour later we were shaking hands with an officer from the West Yorkshire Regiment and what a welcome we received.

Then they led us for a wonderful meal and real tea and a drink of rum. We finally sat down around the fire to tell our story and to hear the news from home; that night we went to sleep knowing we were safe again for the first time in years. The date was May 1st (1945) [possibly 29/30 April], three years to the day since we left home. We shall never forget the kindness and hospitality shown to us everywhere we went, but the final seal for all of us was when we heard the good news of our parents at home. It was good to hear that those who were left behind in the camp at Rangoon Jail all got back safely home.

Now, in the hands of their liberators, Frank and the surviving Pegu Marchers were safe. He had made it. He had survived the unforgiving jungle and the raging rivers; he had survived battles, exhaustion, starvation, dehydration, disease and the cruelty of the guards at the camps and jails he passed through. However, he was in a minority and the statistics are grim. Of the 276 Chindit officers and other ranks from Operation LONGCLOTH who were held in Rangoon, just 131 survived. Several of these died within months of liberation.

The village where Frank was rescued is called Waw. I had been unable to find out exactly where Waw was located, but had made some enquiries and found the details of a retirement home in Bago, which was thought by my guide to be close to Waw. My hope had been to find elderly Burmese people who might have memories of the Japanese occupation. The home was a pre-fabricated building. We were met near the entrance by the manager, dressed in a traditional *lunghi* skirt. I was shown into a dormitory to meet the residents.

The room contained a row of beds. Two men sat cross-legged on their beds with a third on a chair and they listened as I explained why I was there. The manager spoke with the men and explained that the oldest among them was in his mid-70s; too young to have any memory of the war. 'Do they know,' I asked, 'if there was a village called Waw nearby?'

There was some discussion between them and one of the men gestured in a direction behind him, which led to a fair amount of head-nodding from the manager and the other men. I was actually on the outskirts of Waw village and could walk to the place, but also there I would find a man in his 80s who had always lived in Waw and might be able to help me.

I was set on the path to the village by the manager. I was now just a couple of hundred metres away. Walking along a red-mud path, past a small golden pagoda, I approached the first house at the edge of the village, bamboo with a grass roof. A villager with a broad smile, wearing an orange T-shirt and a hat fashioned from dried leaves and carrying a scythe came over to me. My guide interpreted. Yes, there was a man in his 80s. He was the oldest man in the village, was called U Chow, and his house was very close.

The homes were all made of teak and bamboo frames with grass coverings. Some were on stilts over a stream that dissects the village. U Chow's home was behind a small fence. A young man sat in front of the house fashioning sticks of wood with his *dah* as another man sat nearby talking with him. A lady carrying a baby stood in the doorway. Explaining the reason for my visit, I was answered with the smiles and warmth I had come to expect in this mysterious land, and invited into their home.

U Chow sat on a mat in the middle of the wooden floor in a white collarless shirt and deep red *lunghi*. He listened with patience as I told him why I was on this journey and why I had come to Waw. I showed him my cherished photograph of Frank in India. He studied it for a while before he began to speak: 'I was a boy at the time of the war.' The Japanese soldiers, he recalled, had been very cruel. They had raped women, would slap people hard in the face and had pulled out the fingernails of some of the men.

He told me that he remembered aeroplanes flying over and dropping bombs. He watched British and Japanese fighter planes in combat. It was terrifying and the villagers all left Waw for a while for the next village where shelters had been dug.

'Did you see any prisoners?'

'No, because I was hiding in the shelters in the next village but we saw the British soldiers and they were all very tall but did not hurt anybody and the men from the villages joined them in fighting the Japanese.'

As I wandered around the village, I was again surrounded by locals who wanted to see the strange man who had suddenly appeared. I was told I was the first Westerner to go there since the war. Seventy-two years earlier my grandfather was liberated in this village. Seventy-two years ago, my grandfather and his comrades became free men. Against the odds they survived. In this village, with Philip Stibbe who remembered Frank as the prison tailor, Denis Gudgeon who bore testimony to Frank's gut-wrenching task of stitching bodies into sacks, Ras Pagani who sat by and prepared the bodies for those sacks. With Dr Ramsay and Dr MacKenzie who in the most adverse conditions had saved so many lives. With two other Jewish Chindits: Leon Frank, whose morale and sense of humour could not be broken, and Ellis Caplan who lived just down the road from Frank in Manchester, which they would live to see again.

The next day, the men helped each other along and were collected by ambulances to be taken to the Allied rear lines, away from the fighting. Along the way, they saw the devastation of war. They saw Japanese snipers tied into the trees, all dead. The Japanese army was gone, in full retreat or in increasingly reduced forces, making their final stands in their determination to die for the emperor.

Frank embarked on Her Majesty's Hospital Ship *Karapara* at Rangoon bound for Calcutta. For the first time in his life, Frank boarded a plane, a Dakota, and was flown to Akyab Army Base and then to hospital in Comilla. Eventually, he was strong enough to travel home. I do not know how he got back. There was no ceremony; just a pass home and a discharge certificate. The certificate, dated 15 November 1945, attests to 5 years and 205 days of service and that his military conduct was 'very good'.

On 11 May 1945, Frank's mother received a knock at the door. She was handed an official envelope. Trembling, suddenly numb and fearing the worst – the news she had dreaded for two years – she opened it.

Dear Mrs Berkovitch,

It is with very great pleasure that I have to inform you that a report has been received from the War Office that your son is now in Allied hands in Burma; he was liberated on 30.4.45.

He will be brought back to the United Kingdom as soon as transport can be arranged. At present it will not be possible for you to communicate with him, but you may be sure that immediately any further news is received concerning his return to this country, you will be notified.

In a brief announcement in the *Manchester Evening News* on Saturday, 19 May 1945, it was reported that, together with his Chindit comrade Ellis Caplan: 'Pte. Frank Berkovitch (King's Regiment), Greenstead Avenue, Crumpsall has been released from a Japanese prison camp.'

Then, on a cold November day, there was a knock on Sarah's door. She opened it. Her son was home.

Epilogue

'Only the dead have seen the end of war.'

Plato

Sleep did not come easily to Frank, who suffered from nightmares throughout the rest of his life. There was no understanding throughout his lifetime of the effects of stress and psychological distress that were suffered by soldiers and prisoners of war. So he was left to wake up sweating from nightmares. To sit awake on those nights when sleep eluded him, waiting for the distractions brought by daylight, as he thought of the first sighting of Durban, the sights of India, the jungles of Orchha, Abchand and Patharia, of crossing rivers, of cutting through elephant grass, of the battles, the marches – of the hunger, fatigue and fear – and of the faces, the faces of enemy who fell at the muzzle of his Bren, the faces of friends whose lives were cut short in front of him, the faces he nursed on a veranda in a filthy, mosquito-infested jail, and the faces at which he took a final look as he closed them into their hessian coffins.

He belonged to the Japanese Labour Camp Survivors' Association of Great Britain who campaigned for compensation and an apology from the Japanese. It is my hope that through this group, his involvement with the Association of Jewish Ex-Servicemen and contact with other prisoners of war and Chindit comrades, Frank was able to receive some understanding and support from others who had been through similar ordeals.

Under the 1951 Treaty of Peace with Japan, compensation was paid to British prisoners of war. The payment Frank and the other former PoWs received was £76.50. Subsequent British governments maintained that the matter of compensation was now closed. In 1998, the then Prime Minister Tony Blair met with the Japanese Prime Minister Ryutaro Hashimoto who offered 'an expression of deep remorse and heartfelt apology to the people who suffered in the Second World War.' It fell far short of the apology from the entire Japanese government that former prisoners of war had hoped for.

I think I finally understand why Frank did not talk. How could anyone who had not faced the horrors he had survived possibly understand? Only those who were in the jungle or the jails can have known. As best as he could, Frank got on with his life. He married Millie, after whom I have named my daughter, and my son is named after him, bearing the same Hebrew name 'Ephraim'. He had two sons and for the rest of his life he remained in Manchester, frequenting the synagogue, working as a tailor and never again travelling abroad.

Each Friday, I would go to collect Frank to bring him to my parents' house for our Sabbath meal. He stood at my side, and the sides of my brothers, at our Bar-Mitzvah coming-of-age ceremonies and would sit each year at the Passover feast, surrounded by family, as we told the story of the Exodus of the Jews from slavery, a story that must have resonated with him. At times like that, I believe he would silently nod to himself and with deserved satisfaction think 'I made it.'

Appendix I

The Memoir of Frank Berkovitch

[NB: The following appears verbatim with no editorial intervention.]

Chindit, the name given to Orde Wingate's troops in the Burma operations. The Chinthe is a mythical animal, half-lion and half a flying Griffin, it sits at the entrance to Burmese Pagodas to ward off evil spirits.

This authentic and moving recollection is of the high tension of the Wingate Expedition into Burma and behind Japanese lines in 1943. I remember and recall from my own knowledge, the magic of his influence and impact, which seemed to inspire the men. He was a very striking and highly unorthodox character for the way he persuaded the War Office and the High Command to try what was called, Long Range Penetration into enemy territory and harass the enemy and cut their communications.

The moment Wingate got up to speak he did not have to search for words. He knew exactly what to say about the great possibilities of this type of warfare, of Long Range columns of men behind enemy lines. If ever a man had risen to an occasion, it was Wingate; there is no doubt that Wingate was a man of powerful intellect, courage and determination. I was convinced he was a man of destiny, his missions into Palestine and Abyssinia and the successful infiltration of Burma had certainly shown this.

The Japs and the jungle were no obstacle for his organized infantry, his forces achieved great tangible results, showing that British troops could operate in the Burma jungle as effectively as the Japanese. Of the other men under his command, the nearest to Wingate in his views on the war in Burma was Major Mike Calvert. He had the talent for irregular warfare, for training guerrillas and commandos and the job of attacking the Japanese behind their own lines. Calvert was a natural rebel, but was full of ideas on irregular warfare; he had a great sense of humour and the wonderful zest for combat.

Memories of my first night in the jungle were not good ones. No sleep was possible, with the noise of the shrieking birds and rustling in the undergrowth, all sounds alien to a city boy. Next morning we had a lecture from Wingate and every point was driven home in his own convincing way, about our commitments to take part in the recapture of Burma. Our job was to penetrate behind the enemy lines, to create havoc and to distract the Japs and cut all lines of communication.

We would be supplied by air drops at designated sites (SDs). We achieved great results in Burma and the operation made an enormous impact, showing that the British troops could operate in the Burma jungle as effectively as the Japanese. There would be many strange tales of hunger and a feeling of exhaustion from the men in Burma and none of the wounded would return. But we had the courage to see things through and we learnt to respect Wingate and admire him for his interest he had for all his men.

Wingate was supremely self-confident, with ruthless and unorthodox ways and a very domineering element in his character and methods. But he could be very gentle in giving orders to his men as they harassed the enemy with their guerrilla attacks and penetration well behind the Jap lines.

The Chindits infiltrated deep into Burma, laden down with a seventy pound pack and Bren gun and fighting many actions along the way. After we collected a successful air drop [1] we then marched hard and moved forward to attack a Jap Garrison at Pinbon. We blew bridges behind us, then through the village of Tatlwin and on to Nankan where we blew up the railway and then we crossed the Irrawaddy.

We then got the orders to pull out in small parties so we would be sure that many of the men would reach India and get the information back where it mattered. My party moved south to the Irrawaddy and tried to cross. There was just one boat, which took half the men over while we waited for the boat to return. The current was too strong for two men to bring the boat back, so the rest of us marched on for about seven miles to another village, but found the Japs there. We moved back into the jungle and then moved on through with little hope of getting out of Burma.

With all our food gone and very little water left we were exhausted from moving through the thick jungle and found our progress was very slow. After a short rest we moved on again and came upon tracks of an elephant, which we followed to a pool of filthy water. We put some in our mess tins and boiled the water before we drank it. We then moved on and came to another village, but we did not approach the village right away in case there were any Japanese there.

After a while we started to move forward very slowly, our Sergeant [2] was leading us in front, then from out of nowhere the Japs seemed to spring out from everywhere. Many of the men were wounded and the Sergeant got killed, with the rest of us captured. They tied our hands behind our backs and took all our possessions. They then marched us to a camp called Hintha, then started to interrogate us, but there was little that we could tell them. The Japs then marched us, still with our hands tied behind our backs to a place called Nampaung; they placed us in cages and made fun of us.

Later, we were driven by lorry to a jail in Bhamo. In the jail we saw many more prisoners including Gurkhas. The sanitary conditions were awful with no medical facilities at all for the wounded. At night we lay on bare floorboards, the days seemed to drag on, but we rested at night.

We were then told to march once more. It was very hard for we were very weak from lack of food. The little rice and vegetables was not enough to give us the energy to carry on. We were in a shocking condition, but the threat of being shot if we fell out (kept us moving), where we got the energy from to carry on, only God knows. We prayed while we marched because without God's help we would not have survived.

We were in a state of exhaustion, but we still carried on, the Japs put some of the worse cases on the ration lorries and the rest of us marched on into the Shweli Valley. By the time we arrived at Lashio we were in a very bad state. We were herded into cattle trucks and sent on our way to Maymyo. We hoped that when we arrived there the Japs would treat us a little better, but it was not to be. The guards carried clubs, which they were very fond of using on the prisoners for the slightest reason.

I saw a pal (of mine) hit by the Japs and then kicked in the shins till he couldn't walk; it was like being on the edge of a volcano. The treatment in the camp was really rough and very painful at times. They would beat us when we did not bow to the sentry in the camp. Then more prisoners were brought into the camp and dysentery broke out, but the Japs did not help us and conditions deteriorated and lots of our boys died.

After many months there (Maymyo Camp) they started to move us to the railway, then placed us in cattle trucks with sentries to guard us. It was impossible to sit down with so many men in one truck, but at last we arrived at Rangoon Jail where they opened the gates and marched us into the compound.

We found lots of our men from the Brigade in the camp; also, many officers, life in the jail was very bad. Roll call took place morning and night; we had to fall in on parade and with the words of command in Japanese were called to attention, then gave our (POW) number in Japanese. Numbers like Ichi-nee-san-go, then eyes right and then bow. You got beat up if you did not bow to them we worked like slaves.

We lost a lot of wonderful men in the camp for the lack of good food. When we went out on work parties we would try to bring food from outside, but we got caught by the Japs and they beat us across our legs and face. We were losing a lot of men from the bad food, many died every day and you did not know if you were next. Those that had dysentery became so weak; I would not like to describe the filth and stench from the dysentery. When out on working parties the men got scratched or grazed on their legs and arms, which then developed into septic ulcers which slowly rotted the flesh away. Things got so bad they sent a Dr Ramsay to our part of the camp (Block 6).

He (Ramsay) got some medicines to help him, the men on working parties found some bluestones and brought them back into the camp and gave them to Dr Ramsay. He grounded the bluestones and made them into a paste to put on the jungle ulcers. My word he saved a lot of men, even though he was deprived of any drugs to work with, still he reduced the death rate in the camp.

The disease that claimed a lot of men was beri beri. This disease attacked the men in the form of chronic diarrhoea, the man got thinner, whilst others swelled-up from the feet upwards, working its way through the body, this caused fluid under the skin and they became inflated with water. About 70% of the Wingate Brigade (that became POWs) died in the camp.

There was a cholera outbreak in the camp (mid-June 1944) and Dr Ramsay risked his life looking after the sick. This was a terrible time for us, for you never knew who was going to be the next victim of this disease. The Japanese were very worried for themselves and so Dr Ramsay was given medical supplies and drugs to help with the cholera disease and thank God the epidemic was checked, but not before many men died.

Finally, about midday on the 25 April (1945), we were told that all fit men; both British and American prisoners would be leaving for an unknown destination. At this hour the Japs produced large amounts of food for us on the long march. We all felt that all our hopes for an early release were shattered and we would possibly be shot before our troops arrived in Rangoon. The wounded and sick stayed in the camp with a few guards and we hoped they would be ok.

I can only describe the pathetic sight, some of us had homemade sandals, but most of us in bare feet, we marched all day, we were exhausted and footsore. We rested for a short time in an area subjected to bombing as we were near Prome Airfields. It was not safe to move by day, at nightfall we marched to a junction near the Prome Road and then marched through paddy fields and by a village near Pegu. One officer took ill and we never saw him again, probably the Japs shot him.

We marched again at night; many more fell out of the march and were never seen again. We were resting at the side of the road when we heard aircraft overhead, then we heard heavy explosions from the area of Rangoon and were worried about our lads back in the camp. We then pressed on towards Pegu; we could see the glow in the sky not far from Rangoon. Our feet were very sore and it was agony to march. Words cannot convey the mental torture we were going through, the rest was a prolonged torture we were going through in aching bodies.

The Japs were in a very awkward predicament, with our troops moving in (Fourteenth Army) and the Japs trying to get out with the prisoners to a safe place. We did not know where they were taking us; suddenly our planes came overhead during the day and fired their guns as they swooped down on us, being very suspicious of our movements. Words cannot convey the nervous strain put on us, for to be machine-gunned from our planes would be the last straw.

They must have thought we were Japs and we were lucky very few were wounded and killed from the machine gun bullets and cannon fire. We spent the rest of the day hiding in a nearby wood and thinking about the possibilities of escaping, but wondered what chance we would have with the attitude of the Burmese towards us, for they were all for the Japs.

We marched on, everything seemed like a crazy dream. We were weary and footsore and some of the men could not carry on any further, the Colonel [5] told the Japs that the men could not march anymore and persuaded the guards to let us rest in the woods. The cooks were busy getting some food and hot drinks for the men and the Japs let us rest up for the rest of the day. Suddenly, someone shouted out for us to pay attention while Colonel Power made an announcement.

We all turned towards our Colonel, we did not dream what was coming next. Then we heard in a clear voice that everybody could hear that we were all free men. There was an audible gasp from the men, and then some were weeping and laughing, we went crazy with joy, shaking and hugging each other. The Japs had left us; we were advised to stay where we were as our own troops were advancing from the north. However, we were caught up with the Japs trying to get out of Burma and our troops coming in fast; we found ourselves in a very bad spot, we were free, but in great fear.

When some semblance of order was restored we decided we would try and make contact with our own troops. Using all available white clothing and some help from the Burmese, who had now turned on the Japs, I made a Union Jack in record time and laid it out in the paddy field. We hoped that this would show that we were British prisoners of war, just released by the Japanese and they would send us food, a wireless transmitter and medical supplies.

We then heard shelling bombardments in the distance, it must be our troops advancing, then several planes came over very low and must have seen our message and reported back to Head Quarters. From what we were told later on, they thought it impossible that we were prisoners of war and thought it was a Japanese trick they were pulling. So the planes came back and bombed and machine-gunned us as we hid behind some large trees.

Several men clung together in deep holes trying to (protect) ourselves as the planes came back again and again. At last the planes returned to base, a lot of men were killed, but we could not blame our Airmen for they thought we were Japs. How could they know that 400 British and Americans had suddenly appeared out of the blue in no-man's land? They assumed we were Japs, it was very cruel that anyone should have been killed during his first hour of freedom and the tragedy hung over us all.

Our one objective was to get away before the accursed planes returned, we moved back over the paddy fields into a village. The Headman of the village said that there were still Japs around, but the Burmese were hunting them down. This was soon confirmed when rifle fire was heard not far from us. It was very important we try and contact our troops so a Burmese guide and Major Lutz went to try and make contact. They started out up a gentle slope, when suddenly out of the darkness a tense command rang out, our American Major replied and we then knew we were safe.

Figures appeared from the darkness and grasped us by the hands; we moved in a kind of dream, the officer in charge of the patrol told us not to worry as his men would take good care of us. We were told to keep our heads down as there was still firing going on, they then told us that the war was over back home and that the war would not last long in Burma for our lads were moving fast through the country.

We were thrilled to be free again after all the horrors we had been through and in a kind of dream. We moved on and came to some lorries waiting for us out and away from the Japs and toward our lines. One hour later we were shaking hands with an officer from the West Yorkshire Regiment and what a welcome we received.

Then they led us for a wonderful meal and real tea and a drink of rum. We finally sat down around the fire to tell our story and to hear the news from home; that night we went to sleep knowing we were safe again for the first time in years. It was May 1st, three years to the day since we left home. We shall never forget the kindness and hospitality shown to us everywhere we went, but the final seal for all of us was when we heard the good news of our parents at home. It was good to hear that those who were left behind in the camp at Rangoon Jail all got back safely home.

Signed:

FRANK BERKOVITCH

Appendix II

The Prisoners who remained in Rangoon Central Jail after 25 April 1945

The prisoners who were too sick to march were held in Rangoon and for the next couple of days, prison routine continued as normal, with twice-daily *Tenko*. On 29 April, the prisoners found the guards had gone. Two notes were left by the final commandant, Haruo Ito. One note was for the liberating force:

Gentlemen,

Bravely you have come here opening prison gate. We have gone keeping your prisoner safely with Nipponese knightship. Afterwards we may meet again at the front somewhere. Then let us fight bravely each other.

The second note was to the prisoners:

To the whole captured persons of Rangoon Jail. According to the Nippon military order, we hereby give you liberty and admit to leave this place at your own will. Regarding food and other materials kept in the compound, we give you permission to consume them, as far as your necessity is consumed.

We hope that we shall have an opportunity to meet you again at the battlefield of somewhere.

We shall continue our war effort eternally in order to get the emancipation of all Asiatic Races.

Although most of the British men who stayed behind were sick and/or wounded, the fit Indian and Gurkha soldiers had not been included in the march out. Many of them were fit and worked to assist those who needed help.

Some 668 men now remained in the prison. They were also quickly organized into a defensive force by Wing Commander Lionel Hudson, a US pilot who describes the last days in his diary *The Rats of Rangoon*, assisted by the Chindit hand-to-hand combat instructor John Kerr. They feared that Japanese troops may choose to attack them. Guards were posted and a British flag was raised.

News came from Burmese locals that the Japanese had abandoned the city. Hudson met with a major of the Burmese Defence Army, which had now switched sides, and managed to obtain from them grenades, small arms and .303 rifles.

Desperate for medical supplies and to warn the bombers over Rangoon that the jail was now in the hands of the prisoners, messages were painted on the roof of the building: 'JAPS GONE' and 'BRITISH HERE'.

Two days later, as the Fourteenth Army closed in on Rangoon, crack Gurkha paratroopers parachuted in to close off the port and Indian troops arrived in landing craft and charged up the muddy banks to take the Rangoon docks. The Japanese had now abandoned the city.

A British Mosquito plane bombed the wall behind the Block 6 compound, injuring some men. The men were concerned that he thought that the messages on the roof were a Japanese trick. They thought up a message that no Japanese soldier would know and that would prompt the British to 'pull their finger out' and come to their rescue, and so 'EXTRACT DIGIT' was painted on the roof.

The city of Rangoon was eerily quiet. The men looked up and saw a B-24 bomber directly over the jail. Unlike the Mosquito, this was a heavy bomber. They did not even dive for cover. It was all over. The bomb hatch opened, but it was not death that was dropped. It was life. It was rations and medical supplies.

Just a couple of hours later, a force arrived from the Royal Navy. Over the next few days, the surviving prisoners who had remained in Rangoon were evacuated by hospital ships and Dakotas.

Appendix III

The Sad Fate of Michael Calvert

Calvert would return to the jungles of Burma in the second Chindit expedition, Operation THURSDAY, where he again played a critical role. He would go on to join and command the fledgling Special Air Service in desert raids in Africa and then was called on to advise on fighting communist guerrillas in the jungles of Malaya, forming the Malayan Scouts (SAS).

Without doubt, in a time of soldiers, he was of the elite. Yet the ending for Calvert was an unhappy one. In 1952 this great fighter, a true war hero, the recipient of the Distinguished Service Order with Bar, the Belgian Croix de Guerre and the US Silver Medal, was accused of homosexual acts and court-martialled and dishonourably discharged. Calvert vehemently denied the offences for which he had been discharged until he died, but his achievements and courage were no match for the prejudices of the time.

He was unable to fit in anywhere after leaving the army. For a time, he even lived homeless on the streets of Glasgow. In poverty in 1998, months before he died, desperate for money, he sold his medals.

Of the many stories I have read of the men who fought with Frank, this one has left me with the greatest sense of outrage. A sad indictment of the times in 1950s' Britain, no doubt, but worse than this, that he died as he did: forgotten, poor, forced to sell the medals he had so bravely earned. That was in the 1990s and that was how Britain allowed its war heroes to end up. Writing this, I wish I could say that such shameful neglect of veterans, particularly those who had served on the front lines and even behind enemy lines, was consigned to the last century. Sadly, I cannot: homelessness, untreated traumas and suicides continue to haunt ex-servicepersons and government after government has failed to redress these neglects.

Appendix IV

Orde Wingate

Born in India in 1903, Wingate was the product of missionary parents who belonged to the deeply religious, evangelist Plymouth Brethren. The young Orde was imbued with a sense of good and evil, fear of sin, mistrust of extravagance and a belief that all he did would be weighed up on Judgement Day. His childhood was not simply a time of religious instruction, but it is plain, as is so often the case, that his parents' examples and requirements of him resounded throughout his life; he was taken on long walks through hilly countryside and encouraged to gain an understanding of the natural world. The Wingate children were taught to explore, to observe and to be self-reliant.

When he was a pupil at the notoriously tough, spartan public school of Charterhouse, he was again quite an outsider. It was here, according to Royle, that Wingate first met a Jew and remarked: 'I looked at him with the greatest interest and I thought, how extraordinary! There is somebody who is a descendant of David.'[1] Indeed, Wingate went on to be one of the greatest friends the Jews had in the years that followed. In Israel he is a legend, and his name is spoken with reverence by many older citizens. A close friend and confidant of Israel's first president, Chaim Weizmann, and responsible for training future Israeli Defence Force commanders including Moshe Dayan and Yigael Yadin. An elite sports academy, the Wingate Institute in Netanya, is named in his honour.

It was at Charterhouse where he received his first taste of the military, enrolling in the cadets. Wingate, having been born in 1903, was still at school at the time the war ended. Despite the slaughter in the fields of France and Belgium, the staggering losses at Gallipoli and the shift towards peace between nations, Wingate opted for a military life and in 1921 he enrolled at the Royal Military Academy. He did not fit in, being untidy, detached and non-conformist.

His first major posting was to the Sudan where, needless to say, he failed to fit in, at least at first. Quick to state his firm religious views, showing sympathies to Marxism and with his now trademark untidiness, he won few friends among the small group of British officers; however, over time he became more accepted. While he lacked the accepted social graces of the army, he nevertheless learned vital lessons on which he would build and develop through his various commands. With a large degree of autonomy, covering huge areas of desert land, he commanded native Sudanese and Egyptian men and communicated with them in Arabic, having learned it during his posting in the Sudan. He developed an affection for his charges at a time when many racial divides were far more pronounced than today and when many of his peers would have seen the native forces as inferior. Despite his warm feelings towards his men, his firm but fair approach was such that he did not hesitate to use corporal punishment against those who breached his rules or committed any criminal act.

It was while tasked with catching poachers and criminal gangs on the Ethiopian border that Wingate gained first-hand experience of patrolling, not just as an effective way of hunting their quarry but in training and developing soldiers, in navigating, working together and being alert. The seeds were planted that would grow into his unshakeable belief that ordinary men, with little or no experience of soldiery or combat could be trained to be reliable soldiers, capable of fighting in hostile environments.

Wingate used his time in the Sudan developing as a soldier and testing his limits: learning to navigate by stars in the wilderness, camping alone on the Blue Nile and hunting and foraging for his own food and taking long solo treks without food or water. His contemporary Leonard Mosley, in his book *Gideon Goes to War*, said that Wingate 'regarded the Ethiopian frontier as a training ground upon which he could work out the theories of guerrilla warfare which were already working in his brain.'

It was in the Sudan that Wingate was hit by dark bouts of depression, at a time when there was precious little understanding of this debilitating disease. Describing it as a 'blackness' that clamped down on him, 'the temptation of Satan' to destroy himself, these fits would last two to three days and would haunt him throughout his life.

The posting to the Sudan, while certainly an adventure, was while he was still a junior officer and, compared to his peers, he was still relatively inexperienced. His next posting was entirely different.

Wingate arrived in Palestine in 1936. Becoming fluent in Hebrew, he became firm friends with a number of Zionist leaders in the provisional Jewish leadership.

Keen to support Jewish settlements, his Special Night Squads of British soldiers and Jewish fighters fought numerous engagements and carried out ambushes on unsuspecting Arab militants. He was shot five times in a battle with an Arab gang and continued to give orders, yet they still enjoyed success after success. This proved to him that small groups of well-trained, committed and properly-led men, with good intelligence, could do far more effective damage than a large standard force.

Yet despite his successes, British policy was shifting towards appeasement of the Arabs as war with Germany looked increasingly likely. Jewish immigration was further curtailed, a plan to divide the land into a Jewish state and an Arab state was announced and the policy of training and arming Jews was halted. Wingate was returned to England and, in order to keep him away, his passport was marked as not valid for Palestine.

The next posting seemed to be tailor-made for Wingate: a return to Africa, to the Sudan and Ethiopia, to work with native troops under the stars and for a cause, to reinstate Emperor Haile Selassie, Lion of Judah, on his throne.

Wingate, unlike T.E. Lawrence, was not inclined to offer great rewards or promises of arms and money to those he sought to enlist. He preferred to tell locals that he was going to fight and, if they shared his cause, they were welcome to join and prove themselves, much as he had with the Special Night Squads.

Wingate's force consisted of about 1,600 patriots supported by 70 British officers and NCOs, armed with mortars, Bren guns and rifles, heavily outnumbered by the overwhelming size of the Italian force of 35,000 men. Creating a force around him that he felt he could rely on, he named them 'Gideon Force'. Wingate was not fighting with numbers; he had instilled in his officers and NCOs the need to adopt guerrilla tactics if they were to win, focusing on stealth, silence and unpredictability to cut off the main supply road used by the Italians and to move quickly across the land, using deception and ruses to confuse the enemy.[2]

While there were battles fought by Gideon Force, bloody ones, it was by deception that Wingate was able to overcome far larger Italian forces. In one example, his men took the fort at the small city of Debre Markos and a war correspondent, fluent in Italian, used the still-functioning telephone to call each of the forts garrisoned by the Italians along the Blue Nile. Feigning panic, he claimed that there was a huge enemy force closing in on them. The Italians abandoned each of the forts without a fight.

At the beginning of May 1941, the emperor, Wingate and the patriots, bearing the Ethiopian flag, rode into Addis Ababa and after five years of exile, the Lion of Judah was returned to his people.

After repeated orders to attend headquarters in South Africa, which Wingate obeyed only when he wanted to and not with the urgency the orders demanded, he found his conduct had irritated numerous officers. Jealously was also plainly a cause: Wingate had achieved success with minimal resources. He was told to immediately leave for Cairo.

Back in Cairo among the well-dressed staff officers, he was alone, rejected and dejected when he retired to his room at the Continental Hotel. He could be heard shouting, praying loudly and groaning. An officer in the next room heard him shouting, and then a thud. He went to investigate and found Wingate unconscious in a pool of blood, having cut his own throat with a razor. Thanks to the swift action of the officer, Wingate recovered in hospital after a blood transfusion. The recovery was tough as he fought the guilt of what he saw as the temptation of Satan to end his life. His enemies were united in their agreement that this was what was to be expected of a man they had long said was unstable and this would certainly mark the end of his career. Yet again, they underestimated Wingate. Treated by a Jewish doctor who was a personal friend, he recovered fully and sufficiently so that Wavell, in need of an unorthodox commander, requested that he be posted to India in order to plan for a strike back against the Japanese in Burma.

After Operation LONGCLOTH, Wingate returned to Burma with a larger Chindit force in Operation THURSDAY. He was accompanied by Mike Calvert and Bernard Fergusson, as well as a handful of LONGCLOTH survivors.

The operation was a daring and ingenious airborne invasion built on intelligence from LONGCLOTH. In an operation never previously attempted, a force of Chindits, under cover of night, were flown in by glider into pre-arranged landing zones.

Despite losses when some of the gliders crashed, they secured the sites, allowing more troops to land and build airstrips in the clearings among the mountains and jungle. The remainder of the force plus mules, weapons, ammunition and supplies was then flown in by Dakotas.

The plan was for a first wave of gliders to land troops to secure the sites, nicknamed Piccadilly, Broadway and Chowringhee. A second wave would land more troops and American engineers with their equipment to construct an airstrip so that C-47 Dakotas could bring in the remaining troops and equipment. In total, in March 1944, 10,000 men were flown in, all having passed Wingate's gruelling selection test.

The Chindits were involved in numerous ferocious and bloody battles, particularly around Broadway and the fortified jungle bases nicknamed White City at Mawlu and Blackpool near Mogaung. Fighting in the jungle was, like LONGCLOTH, often hand-to-hand.

They continued to harass enemy supply lines and ambush patrols. However, with larger, better-supplied numbers, they were able to re-take territory. Calvert took Mogaung with a huge loss of 800 men. The 23rd Brigade went behind the enemy lines at the Battle of Kohima and made a large contribution to the defeat of the enemy.

Again the men faced exhaustion, thirst, hunger, a committed enemy and the dangers of the jungle. Again, there were occasions when the wounded were beyond help. As the base at Blackpool was abandoned, nineteen Chindits who were too badly injured to move were shot rather than being left to the Japanese.

Outstanding courage was shown by all those who took part. Four Victoria Crosses were won by Chindits in Operation THURSDAY: Captain Michael Allmand, Lieutenant George Albert Cairns, Rifleman Tul Bahadur Pun and Major Frank Gerald Blaker.

By the end of the campaign the Chindits had suffered very heavy casualties with approximately 1,400 killed and 2,500 wounded. Of the survivors, a majority were deemed unfit for further service.

Among the casualties was Wingate. After the aeroplane crash in which he was killed on 24 March 1944, he was buried near Bishnupur. His remains could not be identified as the bodies of all ten men who died in the crash had been too badly burned in the explosion. The bodies were re-interned in Imphal. There were Americans on the flight and the US government arranged for the bodies to be exhumed and transferred to America. Wingate now lies, among soldiers, in Arlington National Cemetery.

Assessment of his achievements is difficult as so many of those who criticized his actions did so out of spite rather than objectivity. For a man who claimed that popularity is weakness, Wingate was as divisive in death as he was in life. In Israel, a country that knows more than most about irregular warfare and reliance on special forces, the man to whom they gave the honorific title of 'Ha'Yadid' ('The Friend') is seen as a military genius, ahead of his time and the founder of the Israeli Defence Force. Maybe there was an insanity of sorts, as is found in the no man's land between madness and genius, or maybe he was simply different and sufficiently certain of his beliefs that his denigrators felt the need to give him a label. Without doubt he was a visionary, highly intelligent and of remarkable personal courage. This was a man who marched at the head of his army and into danger on numerous occasions and set the bar for leading by example. He fought depression but contrasted this with a sense of self-assurance that caused men like my grandfather, a humble tailor, to be prepared to follow him through the gates of Hell.

Endnotes

Chapter One
1. Walsh, J., niece of Private Arthur Almond, Brigade Column, in correspondence with Stephen Fogden, chinditslongcloth1943.com

Chapter Two
1. Van Creveld, M., *Moshe Dayan* (Weidenfeld & Nicolson, 2004).

Chapter Three
1. Shipster, J., *Mist on the Rice-Fields: A Soldier's Story of the Burma Campaign* (Leo Cooper, an imprint of Pen & Sword Books Ltd, 2000).
2. Oura, T. (translation Ogata, D. and Sanwo, F.), *Toshihiro Oura: The Diary of Probational Officer* (Intelligence Section of the US Army's 37th Infantry Division, 08 July 1943)
3. Kazuo, T. and Nunneley, J., *Tales by Japanese Soldiers (Captain Tadashi Suzuki, Gun Company, 215 Infantry Regiment, 33 Division (1942, Sittang, Burma)* (Weidenfeld & Nicolson, 2001).
4. Testimony of Phillips, R.L., missionary, regarding events in 1939, Nanking, in a testimony to the US State Assembly Investigating Committee, December 1943.
5. Calvert, M., D.S.O., *Fighting Mad: One Man's Guerrilla War* (Pen & Sword Military, 2004).

Chapter Four
1. War Diary W0172/2516, Box 105 HS/WD/Burma, 13th King's 1943.
2. Oral History of Frank, L., Imperial War Museum, 19.09.1995.
3. Diary of Lieutenant Wilding, R. from the collection of Stephen Fogden.
4. Chinnery, P., *Wingate's Lost Brigade: The First Chindit Operations 1943* (Casemate Publishers, 2010).
5. Burchett, W.G., *Wingate's Phantom Army* (Thaker & Co. Ltd, Bombay, 1944).
6. Fergusson, B., *Beyond the Chindwin* (Fontana Books, 1955).
7. Calvert, M., D.S.O., *Fighting Mad: One Man's Guerrilla War* (Pen & Sword Military, 2004).
8. MacHorton, I. and Maule, H., *Safer Than A Known Way* (Odhams Press Ltd, 1958).

9. Fergusson, B., *Beyond the Chindwin* (Fontana Books, 1955).
10. Whitehead, J. (director), *Narrow Escapes of WW2: Wingate and the Chindits* (2012).
11. Halley, D., *With Wingate in Burma, being the adventures of Sergeant Tony Aubrey of the King's (Liverpool) Regiment during the 1943 Expedition into Burma* (William Hodge & Co. Ltd, 1945).
12. Thompson, J., quoting Lieutenant James H., 3 Column, 3rd/2nd Gurkha Rifles, *Forgotten Voices of Burma: The Second World War's Forgotten Conflict* (Ebury Press, 2010).
13. Oral History of Frank, L., Imperial War Museum, 19.09.1995.
14. Calvert, M., D.S.O., *Fighting Mad: One Man's Guerrilla War* (Pen & Sword Military, 2004).
15. MacHorton, I. and Maule, H., *Safer Than A Known Way* (Odhams Press Ltd, 1958).

Chapter Five
1. Painter, R., *A Signal Honour: With the Chindits and XIV Army in Burma* (Leo Cooper, an imprint of Pen & Sword Books Ltd, 1997).
2. Outline Narrative of Wingate's 77 Inf. Bde, Burma, February, June 1943, Historical Section (India), closed until 1974.

Chapter Six
1. Halley, D., *With Wingate in Burma, being the adventures of Sergeant Tony Aubrey of the King's (Liverpool) Regiment during the 1943 Expedition into Burma* (William Hodge & Co. Ltd, 1945).
2. Redding, T., *War in the Wilderness: The Chindits in Burma 1943–1944* (Spellmount, an imprint of The History Press, 2015).

Chapter Seven
1. Fergusson, B., *Beyond the Chindwin* (Fontana Books, 1955).
2. Stibbe, P., *Return via Rangoon* (Leo Cooper, an imprint of Pen & Sword Books Ltd, 1994).
3. Oral History of Aves, C.A.W., Imperial War Museum, 17.06.1995.
4. Oral History of Neill, D., Imperial War Museum, 10.08.1993.
5. Rooney, D., *Mad Mike: A Life of Brigadier Michael Calvert* (Leo Cooper, an imprint of Pen & Sword Books Ltd, 1997).
6. Fergusson, B., *Beyond the Chindwin* (Fontana Books, 1955).
7. Rolo, C.J., *Wingate's Raiders* (Charles J. Rolo, George G. Harrap & Co. Ltd, 1944).

Chapter Eight
1. Stibbe, P., *Return via Rangoon* (Leo Cooper, an imprint of Pen & Sword Books Ltd, 1994).

2. Seagrave, G.G., *Burma Surgeon* (Victor Gollancz Ltd, 1944).
3. Stibbe, P., *Return via Rangoon* (Leo Cooper, an imprint of Pen & Sword Books Ltd, 1994).

Chapter Nine
1. MacKenzie, Colonel RAMC K.P., *Operation Rangoon Jail* (Christopher Johnson Publishers Ltd, 1954).
2. Norwood, Captain. J.L. & Shek, Captain E.L., *Prisoner of War Camps in Areas Other than the 4 Principal Islands of Japan* (Office of the Chief of Military History, Special Staff, US Army, Historical Manuscript File, 1946).
3. Stibbe, P., *Return via Rangoon* (Leo Cooper, an imprint of Pen & Sword Books Ltd, 1994).
4. Gibson, A., *Guest of the Emperor – The Memoir of Alec Gibson*, reproduced on Fogden, S., chinditslongcloth1943.com
5. Norwood, Captain J.L. & Shek, Captain E.L., *Prisoner of War Camps in Areas Other than the 4 Principal Islands of Japan* (Office of the Chief of Military History, Special Staff, US Army, Historical Manuscript File, 1946).
6. Stibbe, P., *Return via Rangoon* (Leo Cooper, an imprint of Pen & Sword Books Ltd, 1994).
7. MacKenzie, Colonel RAMC K.P., *Operation Rangoon Jail* (Christopher Johnson Publishers Ltd, 1954).
8. Statement of Lieutenant Akio Onishi, The National Archives, WO 235, File 977, p.17.
9. MacKenzie, Colonel RAMC K.P., *Operation Rangoon Jail* (Christopher Johnson Publishers Ltd, 1954).
10. Oral History of Frank, L., Imperial War Museum, 19.09.1995.
11. Kerr, J., *Diary of Lieutenant John Kerr, Rangoon Central Jail* reproduced on Fogden, S., chinditslongcloth1943.com
12. Fogden, S., *Recording of Denis Gudgeon*, Burma, 2008. See also Davies, P., *Lost Warriors – Seagrim and Pagani of Burma, the last great untold story of WWII* (Atlantic Publishing, 2017).
13. Davies, P., *Lost Warriors – Seagrim and Pagani of Burma, the last great untold story of WWII* (Atlantic Publishing, 2017).
14. Oral History of Frank, L., Imperial War Museum, 19.09.1995.
15. Letter from Prime Minister Winston Churchill to Lorna Wingate, 10 September 1944.
16. Tulloch, Major General D., *Wingate in Peace and War: An Account of the Chindit Commander* (History Book Club, with MacDonald & Co., 1972).
17. Boyd, John with Garth, Gary, *Tenko Rangoon Jail* (Turner Publishing Company, 1996).

Chapter Ten

1. Hudson, Wing Commander L., *The Rats of Rangoon* (Leo Cooper, 1987).
2. Ibid.
3. Oral History of Frank, L., Imperial War Museum, 19.09.1995.
4. MacKenzie, Colonel RAMC K.P., *Operation Rangoon Jail* (Christopher Johnson Publishers Ltd, 1954).

Appendix IV

1. Royle, T., *Orde Wingate: Irregular Soldier* (Weidenfeld & Nicolson, 1995).
2. Mosley, L., *Gideon Goes to War* (Morrison & Gibb Ltd, 1955).